Practical Model Management Using CASE Tools

Books from QED

Database

Managing IMS Databases
Building the Data Warehouse
Migrating to DB2
DB2: The Complete Guide to Implementation
and Use
DB2 Design Review Guidelines
DB2: Maximizing Performance of Online
Production Systems
Embedded SQL for DB2
SQL for DB2 and SQL/DS Application
Developers
How to Use ORACLE SQL*PLUS
ORACLE: Building High Performance Online
Systems
ORACLE Design Review Guidelines
Developing Client/Server Applications in an
Architected Environment

Systems Engineering

From Mainframe to Workstations: Offloading
Application Development
Software Configuration Management
On Time, Within Budget: Software Project
Management Practices and Techniques
Information Systems Architecture:
Development in the 90's
Quality Assurance for Information Systems
User-Interface Screen Design: Workstations,
PC's, Mainframes
Managing Software Projects
The Complete Guide to Software Testing
A Structured Approach to Systems Testing
Rapid Application Prototyping
The Software Factory
Data Architecture: The Information Paradigm
Software Engineering with Formal Metrics
Using CASE Tools for Practical Management

Management

Enterprise Architecture Planning: Developing a
Blueprint for Data, Applications, and
Technology
Introduction to Data Security and Controls
How to Automate Your Computer Center
Controlling the Future
The UNIX Industry
Mind Your Business

IBM OS/2 Series

OS/2 Presentation Manager Programming for
COBOL Programmers
Micro Focus Workbench for the Application
Developer
OS/2 2.0: The Workplace Shell—A User's
Guide and Tutorial

IBM Mainframe Series

VSE/SP and VSE/ESA: A Guide to
Performance Tuning
CICS: A Guide to Application Debugging
CICS Application and System Programming
CICS: A Guide To Performance Tuning
MVS COBOL II Power Programmer's Desk
Reference
VSE JCL and Subroutines for Application
Programmers
VSE COBOL II Power Programmer's Desk
Reference
Introduction to Cross System Product
Cross System Product Application Development
The MVS Primer
MVS/VSAM for the Application Programmer
TSO/E CLISTs: The Complete Tutorial and
Desk Reference
CICS: A How-To for COBOL Programmers
QMF: How to Use Query Management Facility
with DB2 and SQL/DS
DOS/VSE JCL: Mastering Job Control
Language
DOS/VSE: CICS Systems Programming
VSAM: Guide to Optimization and Design
MVS/JCL: Mastering Job Control Language
MVS/TSO: Mastering CLISTs
MVS/TSO: Mastering Native Mode and ISPF
REXX in the TSO Environment, 2nd Edition

Technical

Rdb/VMS: Developing the Data Warehouse
AS/400 Architecture and Planning
C Language for Programmers
AS/400: A Practical Guide to Programming and
Operations
Bean's Index to OSF/Motif, Xt Intrinsics, and
Xlib Documentation for OSF/Motif
Application Programmers
VAX/VMS: Mastering DCL Commands and
Utilities
The PC Data Handbook
UNIX C Shell Desk Reference
Designing and Implementing Ethernet Networks
The Handbook for Microcomputer Technicians
Open Systems

QED books are available at special quantity discounts for educational uses, premiums, and sales promotions.
Special books, book excerpts, and instructive materials can be created to meet specific needs.

This is Only a Partial Listing. For Additional Information or a Free Catalog contact

QED Information Sciences, Inc. • P. O. Box 812070 • Wellesley, MA 02181-0013
Telephone: 800-343-4848 or 617-237-5656 or fax 617-235-0826

Practical Model Management Using CASE Tools

Debra L. Hudson

QED Publishing Group
Boston • London • Toronto

This book is available at a special discount when you order multiple copies. For information, contact QED Publishing Group POB 812070, Wellesley, MA 02181-0013 or phone 617-237-5656.

© 1993 QED Publishing Group
P.O. Box 82-181
Wellesley, MA 02181-0013

QED Publishing Group is a division of QED Information Sciences, Inc.

Library of Congress Catalog Number: 92-37320
International Standard Book Number: 0-89435-440-X

Printed in the United States of America
93 94 95 10 9 8 7 6 5 4 3 2 1

Library of Congress Cataloging-In-Publication Data
Hudson, Debra L.
   Practical model management using case tools / Debra L. Hudson.
      p.   cm.
   Includes index.
   ISBN 0-89435-440-X
   1. Computer-aided software engineering.   2. KnowledgeWare.
I. Title.
QA76.758.H83   1993
005.1—dc20   92-37320
                                                                      CIP

This book is dedicated to my husband, David, for his support in the development of this book and his continuing encouragement in my data administration and model management efforts.

Contents

Preface

Computer Aided Systems Engineering (CASE) tool vendors sell their software based on claims of productivity and quality improvements. CASE tool implementation teams are finding that the CASE tools alone do not achieve the improvement figures that their management has been led to expect by the vendor. Instead, it is the tool set in combination with an easily followed methodology, a trained staff, and an approach to efficiently reuse the deliverables of applications development efforts.

Using their CASE tools, today's organizations are developing a wealth of business models and system models as deliverables from the applications development process. If these models can be utilized across applications development projects and can serve as the foundation for maintenance efforts, the total applications development lifecycle can be reduced. In addition, these models can provide a mechanism for improving the quality of the application by facilitating communication, analysis, and design activities. Organizations need to develop an approach to help them manage their models in a way that blends with (1) their approach to systems development, (2) the CASE tools that are in place, and (3) the way in which the CASE produced models are actually used.

This book is designed to explain the principles of model management required in an organization implementing the Knowledge-

Ware tool set. However, the majority of the approaches and techniques apply to users of all CASE tools who build and maintain models for applications analysis and development efforts. These principles will also apply for firms that have begun to implement one of the growing number of repository tools on the market today, since many of the planning steps, standards, and procedures involved in model management will not be automated by any CASE or repository vendor.

The concepts presented reflect over three years of model management experience using the KnowledgeWare CASE tools on a daily basis. Each tip and technique has been proven through use both at my firm and at other firms I have assisted in beginning model management.

Specific examples have been provided throughout the text. These examples are based on the 2.7 and 1.6 release of KnowledgeWare's Application Development Workbench (ADW) under OS/2 and the 5.01 release of KnowledgeWare's Information Engineering Workbench/Mainframe (IEW/MF) products. My organization served as one of the beta sites for the 2.7 release, and all references to this release are based on the 2.7.01 version. These selected situations have been provided to illustrate how a CASE tool can be used in the model management process. Many of the approaches could apply to most of the CASE tools on the market.

The KnowledgeWare tool set was used to create the majority of the diagrams displayed in the text. To facilitate implementation of the model management concepts within the reader's tools, the name of the tool that produced the diagram is displayed with each diagram. For example, information models were created with the Entity Relationship Diagrammer within the Analysis Workstation.

Chapter 1 explains the basic concepts of models and CASE tools. It is intended to provide even the most inexperienced CASE tool user with the background required to begin understanding model management.

Chapter 2 presents the concept of model management, the types of model management, and the major functions involved. CASE tool support of model management is also explained.

Chapter 3 focuses on management of data models. An overview of data modeling is provided, as well as an explanation of the major issues involved in managing data models.

Chapter 4 focuses on management of process models. An overview of process modeling is provided, as well as an explanation of the major issues involved in managing process models.

Chapter 5 describes modeling techniques that can be used to link the data and process models, illustrating how data is used by the business or a system. Model management techniques for these linkage models are also addressed.

Chapter 6 details the activities involved in managing models on a specific project.

Chapter 7 expands these project model management concepts to a corporate level, explaining how to manage models across multiple projects.

Chapter 8 leads the reader through the development of a customized model management strategy. The reader is encouraged to apply the concepts of the earlier chapters to create a strategy consistent with the goals and constraints of the organization.

Chapter 9 discusses the model management staff, its responsibilities, and management's role in model management.

Chapter 10 explains implementation alternatives, based on existing Information Systems functions, that make best use of existing resources while providing solid model management.

It is my hope that this book will enable all organizations using CASE tools to effectively develop and implement a strategy for long-term model management. Due to the constraints of organizational structures, methodologies, CASE tools, and information systems goals, each organization will need to develop its own customized strategy. This book strives to provide the background, guidelines and practical tips necessary to develop such a strategy.

Definition of Models

GENERIC DEFINITION OF MODELS

Models are representations of functions and information in use or planned for use by the organization. These models may be business-oriented and reflect the business activities and information, or they may be information systems-oriented and reflect the functions and data of a specific information system. Both types of models may be enterprise-wide, including all systems or all parts of the business, or may address a subset of the business or its supporting systems. Models may be as detailed as the tasks required to perform a business activity or the processing logic of a program.

Generally, these models are depicted diagrammatically to facilitate ease of understanding. A diagram can often illustrate complex processes, such as the flow of information through the business, more clearly than several pages of textual explanation. However, a model can be as simple as a list of activities or data groupings. For each type of model, there are numerous ways the model may be illustrated. Each approach may be geared toward a different audience and may contain slightly different views of the same basic information.

These models may be developed in many different environments. Traditional model development occurs in the context of an information systems development project. A model may be developed for a new Manufacturing system. Early models may show the major functions of the system and the major data requirements. Later in project development the models may illustrate the detailed processing logic of a program and the specific components of a database.

The business may also use modeling as part of a business analysis effort. Models can be developed that document the current functions performed by the business. These models can then be modified to reflect various options for work redesign. For example, the flow of inventory through a warehouse can be modeled. Variations on this model can be developed to illustrate possible improvements to inventory flow.

Both the business and the Information Systems groups can use models as documentation of existing business activities and information as well as existing Information Systems functions, logic, and data. The model of the inventory flow can assist the Information Systems group in better understanding how inventory flows today and how it should flow in the future. The group will then be able to apply its technical knowledge to recommend ways in which technology can support the improved process. The models for the new Manufacturing system can help the users of the new system to understand its major functions and the information provided by the system.

PURPOSE OF MODELS

Documentation

A primary purpose of models is to document the business and the systems that support the business. Such documentation, especially in graphical form, can provide valuable information to the business on how it operates. Most Information Systems departments have struggled with approaches to effectively document their systems. Models provide a critical part of that documentation.

Understanding the Business

Through the development of business-oriented models, both the business and the Information Systems group can better understand the business functions and the information used to perform those functions. A strong understanding of the business should be the foundation for any Information Systems work performed. These models allow the Informations Systems group to understand how their systems can interact with the business and how they support critical business functions.

Understanding an Information System

System-oriented models help the business and the Information Systems group better understand a specific set of programs and databases. Visually they can identify major system functions, such as Planning and Inventory Control within a new Manufacturing system, as well as detailed system processing, such as the algorithm used for Production Planning. These models also help explain information and its usage within a spccific system and across multiple systems. The business is the user of all information contained by the system and needs to have a good understanding of each component displayed on a screen or report or accessible through end-user computing tools.

Communication Tool Between the Business and Information Systems

The development of models can serve to improve communication between a specific business unit and the Information Systems group that supports it. The business may use the term Order Entry to include the online keying of an order and the subsequent processing of the order. The Information Systems group may see Order Entry as only the keying of the order. The actual processing may be seen as a completely separate function. To further complicate communication, the Information Systems group may refer to the keying process using a transaction identifier or program name such as OE50612. By developing common, business-oriented terminology, communication barriers such as these can be reduced.

The graphical nature of many models also assists communication. Information Systems can create volumes of textual documentation which may not be understood completely by the business groups. Pictures help bridge that communication gap. It may require several pages of text to describe how order information flows from the Order Entry system to the Order Processing system to the Order Fulfillment system. A simple one-page diagram may illustrate this same information in a format that is much more straightforward.

Improving System Quality

From a systems developer perspective, models can improve the quality of systems analysis and design. By visually reviewing the major functions of the system, the developer can easily identify missing components and organize the system structure. When looking at a new Human Resources system from this high level it may be easy to identify that, while hiring and terminating employees can be supported, there is no mechanism for transferring employees. This sort of omission may be difficult to spot easily by searching several pages of a text-based system definition document.

At the design level, the developer can define detailed processing logic graphically, facilitating the identification of omissions and inaccuracies by the developer and other team members. A diagram illustrating the transfer of data between the programs of a system may clearly highlight flaws in data usage that might otherwise not be caught until testing, when program code changes would be required.

By including the business in the review of these models, system quality can be improved further by ensuring that the system will meet the requirements of the business. As mentioned earlier, models can serve as excellent communication aids. The business can use models to identify areas of miscommunication about requirements and can point out changes early in the analysis and design process, long before system implementation.

Improving Business Processes

Businesses are using models of their business processes as the foundation for improving process efficiency. By documenting current activities and modeling new approaches, the business can easily identify current inefficiencies and possible solutions. This has applicability to activity improvement, job redefinition, and departmental reorganization.

Project Team Coordination

Within an Information Systems project team, models can become a means of coordination. They can display a high-level overview of how a system will function so that all team members can understand how their area of responsibility meshes with the entire system. A more detailed model can help the team members understand specific relationships between their activities and those of the other team members.

Cross-Team Coordination

Many of the benefits available with a project team approach are also available across the Information Systems department. Especially in integrated system environments, it is critical that analysts understand the way in which their system integrates with other systems. This understanding facilitates better design and maintenance of integrative processes and data.

Training

Once developed, models can become a training tool. The business can use these models to train new employees on the business itself and specific systems that are in use. The Information Systems department can use these models to train new employees on both the business and the systems they will support. They can also be helpful in training individuals who transfer within the company.

TYPES OF MODELS

Business Models and Information System Models

Two basic types of modeling are business models and information system models. Business models represent the business itself, the information it tracks, and the way in which information is used by the system. It may include both manual and automated functions. Information system models document the automation of business functions, the actual storage of business information, and the automated ways in which the information is accessed.

Data Models and Process Models

Both business and information system models may represent data, processes, or interaction between data and processes. Data refers to the information that is used by the business. Data models may be high-level representations of data groupings, such as major types of sales information of interest to the business, or detailed file specifications, identifying all data elements captured from the point of sale terminal.

Process refers to the activities that are performed by the business or the system. Process models can also vary in detail, from an identification of the major business divisions of an organization to detailed specifications that explain the logic of a specific program.

Linkage of data and process refers to how information is used in the business or in a specific system. Linkage between these types of models can also be tracked at different levels. A matrix-type cross reference may illustrate the departments that use sales information. Detailed data access may be described specifications, such as the retrieval of sales figures by the point of sale transmission program.

Current Models and Future Models

As well as differing in their scope and focus, models may also represent different time frames. Models developed as a part of a planning project may represent a future view of the business and its information. Information system models may depict the business and the supporting system as it will work when the system is implemented. Current models document the business and information systems as they exist at present.

Conceptual, Logical, and Physical Models

Models can also differ in the level of detail they include. A conceptual model is developed at a very high level, documenting major functions or data groupings. A logical model is at a lower level of detail. It may include an identification of the data elements in a data model or the detailed business activities in a process model. The physical model adds the technical requirements for the system or the database to the basic business requirements identified in the logical model.

In the development of a purchasing system, the conceptual models may identify how information flows within departments and to and from vendors. The logical models may illustrate the same flow at a more detailed level and may begin to identify how information systems could support the flow. The physical models explain the specific files and programs that will be developed to support the flow identified in the logical model. These files and programs may differ somewhat from the data and process identified at the logical level since they must be designed to work efficiently from a technical, as well as business, perspective.

MODEL DEVELOPMENT APPROACHES

Models Developed by Information Systems

A common approach in the past has been for Information Systems professionals to develop models on their own as a part of an information system development project. The model developer draws on his or her own knowledge of the business or system as the foundation for the model. The business may provide assistance in answering specific questions about the model itself but would not be directly involved in the model development activities.

JAD Sessions

Increasingly, the business community has played an active role in the development of these models. Joint Application Development (JAD) sessions are working sessions between Information Systems and the business community that result in models. Usually a member of the Information Systems department or a trained JAD leader acts as the facilitator for the session. Either the facilitator or a scribe documents the model as it is created by the group.

Whether the Information Systems group actively participates in the model development depends on the nature of the model. For business-oriented models, the Information Systems group may be observers, allowing the business team to create their own model. For models of an information system or its data, the business team will identify the requirements while the Information Systems group provides technical guidance.

Business-Led Model Development

After seeing the success of models in an Information Systems environment or as a result of seeing other organizations' successes, the business community is beginning to utilize models as a part of their own business analysis efforts. They may be developed to assist in planning, reorganization, or process improvement efforts. The business may develop the models themselves or they may enlist the assistance of a trained model developer within Information Systems to serve as the model development facilitator.

Reverse Engineering

In addition to these interactive model development techniques, models can also be developed for existing functions or information. This technique is often called Reverse Engineering. The term refers to the concept that system development can be seen as the process of engineering a system. This process includes basic phases of Planning, Analysis, Design, and Construction. Each phase has its own set of deliverables. The deliverables of the construction phase are the programs and physical data structures, such as files or tables. Reverse Engineering is then the transformation of these construction deliverables into models that are deliverables of one of the prior phases.

Reverse Engineering, either manually or with the assistance of automated tools, can provide visual representations of current information systems, the relationships between existing data structures, or current business processes. In addition to providing valuable documentation, these models can provide a starting point for new business analysis or information system development projects.

USING CASE TOOLS TO SUPPORT MODEL DEVELOPMENT

What Is a CASE Tool?

Although models have been in use for many years in the business and Information Systems arenas, it has taken the development of Computer Aided Systems Engineering or Computer Aided Software Engineering (CASE) tools to incite the widespread use of modeling throughout the organization. In this book, CASE will refer to Computer Aided Systems Engineering since the models discussed may document the business itself as well as its supporting systems.

CASE tools assist the systems analyst and applications developer in the analysis of the business and the design and construction of a supporting information system. The purpose of these tools is to automate a part of the manual process involved in the applications development life cycle and to improve the quality of resulting applications.

Types of CASE Tools

Each CASE tool may support different areas of the systems development life cycle. An Upper CASE tool addresses the earlier sections of the project life cycle. Tools that fall into this category may support planning, analysis, and some design activities. Lower CASE tools focus on the later sections of the project life cycle, including detailed design and construction. Some vendors provide integrated CASE tools, often called ICASE, which support both Upper CASE and Lower CASE activities.

In addition to supporting different stages of the project development life cycle, CASE tools may also focus on a different aspect of project development. Some are designed to support only data or database design. Others may provide screen and report prototyping facilities. CASE tool customers have the option of selecting a variety of CASE tools, each with a particular strength, and combining these tools together through purchased or developed interfaces.

This text focuses on the use of the KnowledgeWare tool set. KnowledgeWare is considered an ICASE tool, supporting all facets of the applications development life cycle. The firm's expanding set of tools supports the majority of the activities that occur in each phase of the development life cycle and many of the most commonly used development platforms.

For purposes of discussion in this text, the basic Knowledge-Ware workstations will be the Planning Workstation (PWS), the Analysis Workstation (AWS), the Design Workstation (DWS), the Construction Workstation (CWS), the Rapid Application Development tool set (RAD), and the Documentation tool set (DOC). Other tool sets and workstations are available to support specific applications development functions, such as the definition of systems utilizing the Graphical User Interface (GUI) approach.

In spite of its comprehensive support of the development process, some organizations elect to combine the use of the KnowledgeWare tool set with tools provided by other CASE vendors. These organizations do not receive the true benefits of an ICASE tool set. This text will explain some of the issues facing these organizations. These issues also apply to organizations using any combination of CASE tool vendors available in the industry.

Advantages of Using CASE Tools

The majority of the CASE tools on the market today support applications development activities through some type of modeling. This may be a simple diagram of a flow of data between business functions or a complex model of program logic. By allowing this graphical representation, CASE tools can facilitate communication between the business community and the Information Systems staff as well as communication within that staff. These models can also assist an individual developer in the analysis and design activities by displaying system components graphically at various levels of detail.

Although CASE tools are used to support modeling activities, they also have other potential uses. In the area of database design, CASE tools can automate the generation of a physical database from logical business data requirements. Some can also assist in database tuning activities.

The automatic generation of program code from models, such as screen layouts and specifications, can also provide development efficiencies by reducing total development time and generating optimized code. Developers can then concentrate on the program logic itself, often using a high-level pseudocode language rather than focusing on the constructs of a specific lower-level language. Some tools will automatically create some of the standard screen manipulation code, based on the screen layout and the type of screen specified. The developer may then make only minor modifications to reflect special processing.

Analysis facilities can provide additional development aids throughout the life cycle. In the area of data design, the tool may provide a facility to ensure that a data model conforms to a set of standard data analysis rules, such as normalization. Flows of information can be analyzed by the tool to ensure that all information used by the model can be retrieved from within the documented system.

Benefits of Using CASE Tools for Modeling

Support for specific types of models. The diagramming features within CASE tools were designed to support the development of specific types of models. Therefore, they facilitate both the creation and modification of the models. Some tools also include diagramming logic that performs diagram clean-up logic, such as rearranging boxes to uncross connecting lines. This frees the developer to focus on the content, not the display, of the model.

Additional documentation. In addition to the graphical capabilities, many CASE tools also provide the capability of tracking additional information about objects represented on a diagram. If a developer was using a basic graphics package, a separate word processing document would be required to add additional detail about each of the objects displayed in the model. A CASE tool with enhanced documentation capabilities allows the diagram and the additional detail to be tracked within the same software package, making maintenance of the information easier.

Linkage of models. Most tools also facilitate the linkage of models and detailed information. A model of business activities may be linked to a model of the programs that support the business. For example, the linkage may provide a list of all programs that support Forecasting activities. A model of the data used by the business may be linked to a model of the business activities, illustrating how data is actually used by the business. Such a model may show that Forecasting data is used by Marketing and Production Planning activities. A business process may also be linked to a detailed definition of the process, stored within the same CASE tool.

Integrity checking. CASE tools can also assist the developer in ensuring that a model conforms to standard rules of model development. For example, it can warn the developers trying to add the same data element twice or trying to document the flow of information between two data groupings without identifying a process to perform the flow. These types of integrity checks are based on a rule set which is provided by the tool vendor. This rule set may be specific to a methodology or may provide basic edits which apply across many modeling methodologies.

Tracking of model maintenance. CASE tools can also track maintenance to models. In addition to tracking the creation and last change dates, many tools also track the user identifier of the individual who created the model or made the change. This tracking may be available at a model level or may be specific to individual model components. Advanced tracking facilities track all updates of the model in addition to the last update date. This type of facility can be helpful in tracking model changes and restoring the model to a previous version.

KnowledgeWare provides these benefits to tool set users. Each diagrammer within the tool was specifically designed to make creation and maintenance of the type of model easy for the model developer, while ensuring that basic modeling rules are enforced.

Many options for linking the models are facilitated, such as reference to physical database components within a program specification. The Details diagrammer provides the capabilities of adding description, comments, and some additional descriptive information to different components of models, facilitating the concept of a centralized location of project information. Tool maintenance of creation and last update dates and times and the associated user identifier allows tracking of model maintenance.

HOW CASE TOOLS STORE MODELS

Within CASE tools, there is a centralized storage location, generically termed a repository. This repository stores the components of the model, or repository objects, and information about those objects. The repository tracks all details required to display a diagram and often includes textual notes about the object. It also tracks relationships, or linkages, between objects.

Objects may be any type of information collected in the systems development life cycle or through business planning and analysis. Examples of data-oriented objects include entities, attributes, data structures, and data elements. These objects will be explained in detail in Chapter 3. Business processes, screens, and program modules are possible application-oriented (process-oriented) objects, which will be addressed in Chapter 4.

Linkages identify relationships between these objects. These linkages can show how data is used by an application. A data structure may be referenced in a program specification; a screen may include a data element. It can also show how data objects relate to each other, such as a physical data structure that implements a logical view of data. Process objects can also be related, such as a screen being displayed by a program. Objects can also be related to other objects of the same type. For example, a process may be decomposed into other processes, or a logical data entity may be related to other logical data entities.

Each CASE tool vendor has its own unique approach to what objects are stored, how they are related, and what types of detailed information can be captured. One vendor may store planning information, such as projects, goals and critical success factors. Another vendor may focus only on those objects required for detail design and code generation. Some vendors may capture minimums and maximums about a data relationship, while others only capture maximums.

Vendors also differ in the physical storage medium for their repository. The actual file structure may be any valid storage format, including DB2 tables and sequential files. These files may reside at the workstation, network, or mainframe level. Some CASE tools can use the same repository structure. In other cases, an intermediate file or a common repository is often used as temporary storage to transfer information from one CASE tool to another.

KnowledgeWare has decided to call its repository an encyclopedia. Encyclopedias are databases that consist of four basic files. The object file tracks the existence of each object in the repository and identifies the type of object, such as an entity or a process. The association file tracks linkages between objects. The property file holds details for the objects, including the last maintenance date. The text file includes textual details, such as program specifications. All information collected in the basic KnowledgeWare Workstations is stored in the same encyclopedia and is available to developers working at any point in the life cycle, strengthening KnowledgeWare's position as an ICASE vendor.

In Release 2.7 of KnowledgeWare's ADW software tool set, the files are implemented on a PC platform using a Btrieve database architecture. A mainframe version of the software uses a VSAM structure for storing the same four encyclopedia files. Another mainframe version, to be released by the time this book is published, uses DB2 as its storage medium. Since the mainframe and PC versions of the tool use the same approach to information storage, it is easy to convert information from one platform to another.

2

Why Model Management?

DEFINITION OF MODEL MANAGEMENT

As organizations begin using CASE tools to develop models, small isolated groups develop project specific models. As these groups prove the benefit of models and the viability of CASE tools, more groups begin to use CASE tools to develop project specific models. Eventually, someone needs access to another person's model, either to perform maintenance on the model, to build a new model using the existing model as a starting point, or simply to gain an understanding of the processes or data documented in the model. At this point, the organization needs some form of model management.

Effective model management means ensuring that the correct model is available to individuals within the business and the Information Systems group as needed. This requires making models available to project teams when they begin their projects, incorporating model changes made by the team into the models, and providing models to the business community for information purposes. It may also involve coordination of model usage across projects and the validation of all models to ensure that they accurately reflect the business or system they represent and that they conform to all organizational standards.

Challenges of Model Management

On the surface, this seems like a relatively simple task. It is one that Information Systems personnel have been dealing with successfully for years in the area of program source management. Data administrators have been accomplishing similar tasks within data dictionaries. However, model managers must deal with several unique problems.

First, they must manage many different types of objects with complex relationships. The source manager deals with programs; the data dictionary manager deals with data-oriented objects. Not only does the model manager deal with all these objects, but he or she must also manage all process-related objects, possibly planning objects, and the relationships between the objects.

Second, unlike data objects found in data dictionaries and programs, most model objects have little, if any, agreed-upon standardization. Many of the modeling techniques facilitated by CASE tools are relatively new to the industry. Each vendor supports modeling in a slightly different way. Each methodology may dictate the use of a different set of modeling objects or different object relationships. Each instructor may teach modeling within the same methodology and CASE tool differently. This means the same model could be developed multiple ways. Therefore, determining what constitutes a real change to a model is difficult.

These problems are compounded if multiple tool vendors are used. Suppose Vendor A is selected as the Upper CASE vendor and Vendor B is the Lower CASE vendor. Vendor A's objects focus on the planning and analysis phases of system development. There may also be some objects that support system design. Vendor B's objects may focus on construction but also support design. The model manager must determine how to migrate objects from one tool to another. Even if a conversion package is provided by the vendor, it assumes a certain approach to object usage in both tools. The model manager must be able to ensure that the organization's models conform to the conversion package's models, or must develop a customized conversion.

TYPES OF MODEL MANAGEMENT

Model management can occur at two fundamental levels. Project model management involves tracking the development of models for a specific project. While this level is limited in scope, it poses many daily challenges for the project model manager, who must ensure that valid models are available to all team members as needed. Corporate model management refers to the management of models across all projects in the organization. It also involves management of models that are not currently a part of a project, but are of interest to the organization.

Project Model Management

The purpose of project model management is to provide each developer working on a project with the appropriate information required to do his or her job in the easiest possible manner. This means that each developer needs to have access to a set of models that (1) contains the portions of the project models that are part of his or her responsibility, (2) provides information that help him or her better perform analysis, and (3) includes common information shared by all analysts on a project.

To facilitate this access, project model managers prepare the initial project models from existing models. These models may have been developed as a part of an earlier phase of the same project or as a part of another project. The project model manager then supervises the expansion of these initial models by the development team. This requires that the model manager assign responsibility for specific models or model areas to team members and set the project guidelines for model development. The model manager must be alert for models that need to be shared by team members and must make these models available. At the end of the project, the project model manager should collect all project models and prepare them to be combined into existing corporate-level models.

Corporate Model Management

The primary purpose of corporate model management is to provide and maintain a centralized location of models developed by project teams. This requires making models accessible by all project teams and to the business. If model reusability is a goal of the organization, corporate model management must not only make the models accessible but must also track any changes to these models and share these changes with other model users. This involves a great deal of project coordination activities.

To perform these functions effectively, the corporate model manager must maintain an enterprise-wide perspective. While the project model manager focuses on the needs of one specific project, the corporate model manager must be aware of the goals of the organization and how the models support those goals. Decisions on how to manage all models across all projects must be based on corporate directions and areas of emphasis.

FUNCTIONS OF MODEL MANAGEMENT

Establishing and Enforcing Standards

One of the primary functions of model management is the establishment and enforcement of model standards. To develop these standards, the model manager must first determine what types of objects are required and what types are optional for models. Required and optional relationships between objects should also be identified.

For each of the objects the model manager must identify the information that should be collected. A critical part of this detailed information is the name of the object. For objects that represent physical pieces of the system, the physical naming standards can be used. New naming standards must be developed for other objects. Standards for other pieces of detailed information, such as the standard format for a process definition, must also be considered.

A KnowledgeWare CASE tool user may approach standards by identifying the models that are developed by the organization using the tool. Entity Relationship Diagrams and Process Decomposition Diagrams may identify the use of objects that represent Entities,

Relationships, and Processes. The organization may then define standards for each object. For example, an entity may be required to have a name and a business definition. The name may be defined as a business term with a maximum length of 32 positions. Standard abbreviations may be defined for use in entity naming. There may be no limit defined for business definitions. Optional information may include technical comments for use by the analyst and aliases that identify other business terms for the entity.

To aid in the sharing of models across project teams and business areas, it is often helpful to identify standards for model display. A business process may be represented by a circle, a rounded box, or a triangle. By identifying one standard convention, such as a rounded box for processes, model managers allow all users to easily understand all models developed in the organization that include business processes. By selecting distinct representations, such as squared boxes for data groups and rounded boxes for processes, the model manager can also help avoid confusion about what a model represents.

Once these standards have been identified, easy methods of ensuring that the standards are met need to be developed. To avoid manually checking each object for standards conformance, automated facilitates, either within the CASE tool or as a part of an external tool, should be investigated. These could be in the form of simple reports that scan model information to look for missing details or invalid names.

The KnowledgeWare product provides an exception analysis report that searches for certain types of objects that are missing specified properties, such as definitions or comments. If the organization required all entities to have definitions, the tool could produce a report that listed all processes missing definitions. However, if the organization had customized its use of the textual portion of the tool, perhaps by requiring a technical notes section and an alias section as a part of the comments, the tool would not have an automated mechanism for verifying the existence of these two sections. Instead, the organization could develop a routine that scanned the comments sections searching for this information.

In developing these standards, it is important to consider the limitations of the CASE tools in place. Although the CASE tools should not dictate the standards, they can impose constraints. The most basic example is naming standards. KnowledgeWare limits the names of data objects to 32 positions. The organization may use a different Lower CASE tool that allows only 30 positions for the same data names. The physical database definition tool set may allow only 18 positions. Under this scenario, the model manager may elect to limit data names to 18 positions or may allow 30 positions to be used in KnowledgeWare and the Lower CASE tool. If 30 positions are used, the 18-position name might be contained within the 30-position name or it may be documented as additional detail for the data object.

Establishing the Organization's Information Model

An approach to documenting object-related standards is through an information model. It is a diagram that shows the required and optional objects and relationships for the organization. A more detailed model may also include specific properties, such as name and definition, that are also tracked about an object.

A sample information model is shown in Figure 2.1. This is a high-level information model that will be detailed in Chapters 3, 4, and 5. For purposes of illustration, a simplified entity relationship diagram will be used in this book to diagram an information model. Objects that the organization tracks are identified by boxes. In this diagram, the organization tracks logical data objects, logical process objects, database design objects, and program specifications.

The lines connecting the boxes, called relationships, indicate how the objects are linked together. In this diagram, relationships indicate that logical process objects reference logical data objects, and database design objects are used in program specifications. Logical data objects are implemented by database design objects and logical process objects are implemented by program specifications.

The symbols on the lines indicate the cardinality of the relationship. Cardinalities refer to the number of occurrences of one object that can exist for a single occurrence of another object. The three-pronged symbol closest to a box indicates that for one occurrence of the box furthest from the symbol, there can be many

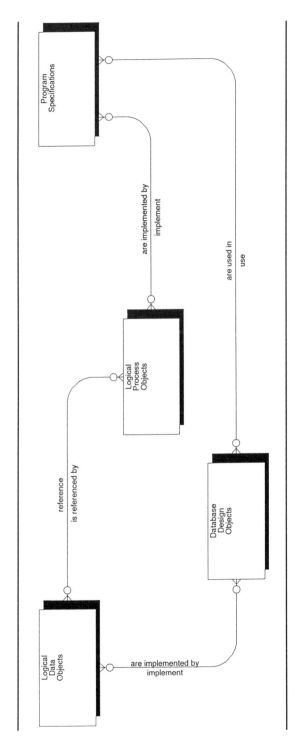

Figure 2.1. Entity Relationship Diagrammer : sample information model.

occurrences of the box closest to the symbol. In this diagram, one
logical data object can be referenced by many logical process objects. If a straight line had appeared on the diagram instead of
the three-pronged symbol, it would indicate that only one logical
data object existed for each process object. The circle next to the
three-pronged symbol indicates that this relationship is optional.
In this diagram, a logical data object can exist without a logical
process object. A line would have indicated that the relationship
was required.

A model such as this can be developed by reviewing the organization's methodology and identifying the deliverables from each
step. These deliverables generally include models. The models
themselves can then be analyzed to identify objects and relationships. A set of questions designed to assist the model manager in
analyzing existing models to develop an information model is provided at the end of Chapters 3, 4, and 5.

In the absence of a defined methodology, the model managers
can review models that are currently produced by the Information Systems group. These models should be evaluated to identify which ones are of value to the organization on a continuing
basis. Once a set of maintainable models is identified, the associated objects and relationships can then be determined.

For an organization wishing to implement the objects and
relationships illustrated in the information model, a supporting
set of CASE tools is needed. If CASE tools are in place that do not
support this model, the organization may need to reassess its
information requirements, consider the implementation of different CASE tools, or design an external facility that stores and
facilitates maintenance of the missing information.

Suppose the organization needs to track detailed program
specifications. If they have only implemented an Upper CASE
tool, such as KnowledgeWare's Analysis Workstation, the information model may highlight the need to consider the purchase of
a Lower CASE tool, such as the Design Workstation. Another
option may be the development of an external set of files, such as
word processing files, that house specifications.

Which direction the organization takes depends on its requirements. First, is a linkage required between the specifications and other models, such as process models developed in the

Analysis Workstation and database definitions, which could also be tracked in the Lower CASE tool? Second, could the organization use some specification analysis, such as syntax checking for pseudocode? Third, is code generation a potential direction for the organization? Since only CASE tools can provide these types of advantages, the additional expense of a Lower CASE tool may be justified.

Establishing and Enforcing Procedures

Once the standards are determined, model managers need to identify how the standards will be enforced. Procedures identify how and when models will be updated. It is also helpful to identify clearly who is responsible for performing the updates. If corporate models are being developed, it is also important to determine how project models will be merged together to form corporate models.

In establishing model maintenance procedures, the model manager needs to identify all possible points where models can be changed. Information Systems development projects are one obvious source of change. Business changes, system maintenance, and planning projects are also possible sources of change. In each of these scenarios, the model manager needs to identify how the model will be changed and who will perform the update. Is the model manager responsible for updating a model if the system changes, or is the individual responsible for making the change? If the model manager makes the actual update, how will the model manager be informed that a change has occurred? This question is especially critical in business models where the business may change and require a model change but the business may not have maintenance responsibility for models.

To track changes to models, model managers can use a variety of techniques, based on the types of facilities provided by CASE tools. If the tool tracks history of detailed changes or provides an automatic compare utility if two versions are available, it may be relatively simple to identify all changes that need to be managed. However, if these types of facilities are not available, the model manager can institute a formal change control process where all changes are tracked by analysts or model managers, perhaps in a change control database. The greatest risk to this manual change tracking approach occurs in situations where analysts can change final versions of models themselves without being required to note the change in the change control database. If the model manager or a primary analyst maintains the final version and only incorporates changes in the change control database, the integrity of the final version can be maintained.

A model manager using the KnowledgeWare tool can use the tool's internal tracking of last update date and the identifier of the user who made the change to determine specific changes that have been made since the last time the model was maintained at a project or corporate level. However, since Release 2.7 of the ADW tool set does not produce a comparison report that lists all information changed since a specific date and time or by a specific user identifier, the model manager may need to develop a special report to obtain the necessary information.

Once the actual update has been defined, the procedures for merging models should be addressed. At a project level, should individual developer models be merged weekly or after a major set of changes? From a corporate-wide perspective, should project models be merged periodically while the projects are underway to identify any potential overlap, or should models only be merged when projects are complete? Should cross-project model merging be performed by project teams or by model managers? How will conflicting models be reconciled? All of these questions should be covered by the detailed model management procedures.

In developing these procedures, the model manager should be familiar with existing project life cycle procedures. If model review and merging can be added to the list of required activities performed at an end-of-phase review, it will be easier to introduce these new activities than if a completely new step is added only to support model management. By making these procedures as much a part of existing procedures as possible, the model manager will reduce the overall resistance that naturally occurs when new activities are introduced.

Establishing the Organization's Activity Model

Model management procedures can also be documented through a model. While the information model documents the types of information to be managed, the activity model documents the steps for managing those models. An activity model may be at a very high level, identifying the major functions to be performed, or at a very detailed level, documenting the procedures themselves.

A sample activity model is shown in Figures 2.2 and 2.3. Figure 2.2 uses a process model decomposition diagram format. A rounded box indicates a function or activity. The lower-level boxes are decompositions, or breakdowns, of the major functions involved in the higher-level box. A 'P' in the lower right corner indicates this is a process. This sample diagram illustrates some of the major activities that occur in model management. Model Management planning would include establishing standards and procedures. Maintain Project Models would involve the project model management activities. Maintain Corporate Models refers to corporate model management activities. Detailed decompositions of each of these functions appear in later chapters.

Figure 2.3 illustrates which portions of the information model are affected by each activity. A dataflow diagram format is used to depict this relationship. The rounded boxes represent processes shown in Figure 2.2. The three-sided boxes are data stores, each one representing an object shown on the information model (Figure 2.1). The double boxes are external agents, in this case representing the individual or group responsible for the activity. The connecting lines indicate a flow of information. The arrow indicates the direction of the flow.

At the level illustrated in the diagram, all portions of the information model are maintained by all activities. As the level of detail increases in both the information model and the process model portion of the activity model, the activities will maintain a more limited number of objects.

There are many ways to organize an activity model. Figure 2.2 considered project and corporate model management as separate activities. Another alternative is to document activities in each phase of the systems development life cycle. The model could also be structured based on the major types of models, such as data models and process models.

The selected approach should be appropriate to the way in which model management is supported in the organization. If

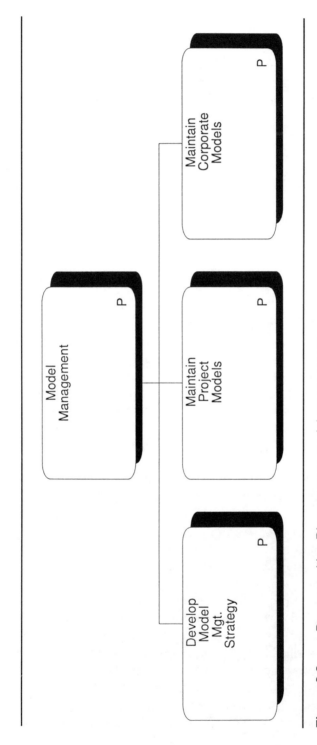

Figure 2.2. Decomposition Diagrammer : model management.

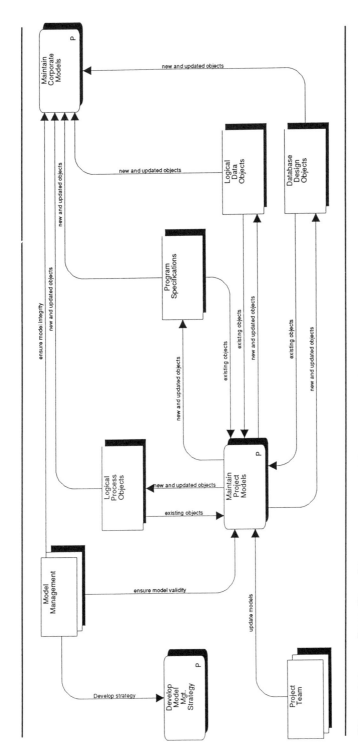

Figure 2.3. Data Flow Diagrammer : model management.

separate individuals are responsible for project and corporate model management, this may be an appropriate breakdown. However, if responsibility is determined based on model type, the data and process model distinction may be helpful. If a CASE tool is being used to develop the activity model, it should be relatively easy to reorganize the model once the support structure has been determined. Sets of questions are provided throughout the remainder of this text to assist the reader in identifying the activities to be included in the activity model and then structuring the model as appropriate.

Tracking Model Updates

Both the standards and procedures should include mechanisms that help track model maintenance. Tracking involves two activities: identifying that a change has occurred and reacting appropriately to the change. Model managers must ensure that all updates that result from the change are completed.

Manual comparison of models is a time-consuming approach to identifying model updates. Most CASE tools provide a last update date and time, which can easily identify a change to a model. The difficult task is identifying the change itself. Few, if any, tools timestamp changes to definitions or names. Instead, the timestamp is on an object or the model itself. If a user identifier is included in the timestamp, it may be easier to identify the change since the individual who made the change can be asked directly. In some situations manual comparison may still be required, but its focus will be greatly reduced by only evaluating those objects that are known to have changed.

Once a change has been identified, the model manager should also ensure that all associated changes have occurred. For example, if a business process has been changed, the programs that support that business process should also be changed. Although the model manager is not responsible for making these changes, he should inform the individuals who maintain those programs that a change may be required. This requires tracking not only the objects themselves but also the linkages between objects and the individuals who have responsibility for maintenance.

HOW CASE TOOLS SUPPORT MODEL MANAGEMENT

CASE tools greatly facilitate model management functions. By providing creation and maintenance dates, CASE tools automatically track model changes. Through internal rule sets, CASE tools can also ensure that some of the standards are implemented. One of the most beneficial ways CASE tools can support model management is through the automated merging of models and model objects and the identification of duplicate objects.

How CASE Tools Merge Models

The majority of CASE tools take one of two approaches to merging models. The first approach, merging based on name matching, relies heavily on naming standards to facilitate model management. The second approach, merging based on an object identifier, places a greater emphasis on procedures to ensure that the correct identifier is maintained through all models. Some tools take a combination of the two approaches, requiring strong naming standards and procedures for complete model management.

Merging based on object name. Object name merging works on the concept of unique names within an object type. For example, a data element named Product Description would be uniquely named across all data elements in a repository. A process called Add a Customer would be uniquely named across all processes in a repository.

To identify a specific object, the CASE tool user would search for a specific name. If a user referenced a specific name that already existed, the CASE tool would assume the user meant the existing object rather than a new one. Therefore, if one model had a program module named PGM0001 and it was merged with another model having a program module named PGM0001, the tool would assume these represented the same object.

Merging based on unique identifier. Other tools may work like many databases, using a unique identifier such as a system-generated number to identify a specific object. This is similar to the concept of a Product Number, a Customer Identifier, or an Order Number. This type of identifier has no real meaning and is intended primarily for efficient access of the object. Just as a list of customer names may be used for ease of customer selection, the tool may present the information to the user by object name instead of identifier. Individual tools differ on whether names must also be unique.

In this type of environment, it becomes very important that, once an object is defined, everyone use that particular instance of the object with its unique identifier instead of creating a new one. For example, if a team is working on a model and needs to use the process Add a Customer, which was created in another model, the team should copy that object with its unique identifier into its model instead of creating a new object representing the same thing.

This is the same approach taken by a Customer Service agent taking a customer's order. Instead of setting up a new customer with a new Customer Number, the agent would first check to see if the customer already existed somewhere on the customer database. This avoids the problem of needing to combine customer information for two customers into one at a later date.

However, just as it is possible in most order processing systems to merge the two customers into one distinct model, objects that are truly the same can be combined in many CASE tools. This merging activity is nevertheless time-consuming and can be avoided by careful management of objects and by use of clear, easily followed procedures for using existing objects.

The KnowledgeWare tool set identifies each specific object by a unique identifier but merges most objects based on identical object names. If two objects have the same name but different identifiers, they are assumed to be the same object, and one of the two identifiers is selected as the single identifier of the new object. The tool's name-matching facility does not consider upper and lower case; therefore, standards do not need to be case-sensitive from a tool perspective.

A merge performed by the tool internally to update physical data models from logical data models is based on the unique identifier rather than on name. This enables a name change in the logical model to result in a name change in the physical model when a merge, here called translation, is requested. More details on the implications of the logical to physical data model translation are provided in Chapter 3. This special merge logic is not available in releases prior to 2.7.

Options for Handling Duplicate Objects

Once a CASE tool identifies a duplicate object, either by identical names or identifiers, the tool needs to determine how to merge the objects. Will a single version be kept and the other version discarded? Will the information from both versions be combined into a single version? Some CASE tools automatically use one approach, while others give the user the option of selecting the merging method.

Selecting a single version. Suppose model A has a definition of the data element Customer Name provided by Marketing and model B has a definition of the same data element provided by Customer Service. If these two models are combined into a single Customer model, either model's definition could become the new definition in the combined model.

Most tools that allow only a single version use the sequence in which the merge is requested to identify the version that remains. The tool may use the first model selected in the merge request as the version to be retained. In the above example, if model A was selected first, the Marketing definition of Customer Name would remain in the merged model. The Customer Service definition would not be seen in the new model (Figure 2.4).

Combining both versions. Consider once again the Customer Name example. Instead of letting the tool select which definition remained, the tool may combine the two definitions. The new definition for Customer Name would include both the Marketing definition and the Customer Service definition (Figure 2.5). The analyst could then modify the definition of Customer Name in the new model to reflect a combination of the two definitions or select the definition that seemed to be most appropriate.

This combination approach may initially be more appealing since no information is lost. However, it has the potential to re-

Marketing Definition

```
The name of the individual in the household to whom all promotional
mailings are sent.
```

Customer Service Definition

```
The name of the individual in the household who generally places
orders.
```

Result if Single Version Selected

```
The name of the individual in the household to whom all promotional
mailings are sent.
```

Figure 2.4.   Merging with Single Version Selected.

Marketing Definition

```
The name of the individual in the household to whom all promotional
mailings are sent.
```

Customer Service Definition

```
The name of the individual in the household who generally places
orders.
```

Result if Versions Combined

```
The name of the individual in the household to whom all promotional
mailings are sent.The name of the individual in the household who
generally places orders.
```

Figure 2.5.   Merging with Versions Combined.

quire maintenance to all duplicate objects. For small models or models with few duplicates, this may be feasible. However, for large models with many duplicates, this manual update could be very time-consuming.

The KnowledgeWare tool allows the model manager the option of choosing the merging method for many objects and properties. The replace option overlays the contents of the target model with the contents of the source model. The combine option merges the contents of both models based on an internal rule set. In using these options, the model manager should be aware that certain objects are always replaced, even if the combine option is selected. Careful attention should be paid to the model consolidation examples provided by the vendor.

3

Data Model Management

TYPES OF DATA MODELS

Data models are representations of information that is of interest to the organization. Although data models are generally thought of as diagrams of data groups and their relationships, data models can actually take any diagram or textual form. A carefully described list of business rules and definitions can provide the same information shown graphically in an entity-relationship diagram.

Conceptual Data Models

A conceptual data model depicts major groupings of data that are in use or will be in use by the organization. These groupings may be called subject areas, data collections, or entity supertypes. Specific data modeling methodologies apply different techniques and rules to these different terms, but the basic principles involved are the same.

Based on the approach taken in conceptual data modeling, the data groups may be high-level abstractions or may represent more detailed data structures. An organization may develop a single data group called PRODUCT or may elect to depict the critical components of product information separately, such as PRODUCT SPECIFICATIONS, PRODUCT ROUTING, and PRODUCT

SELLING FEATURES. Figure 3.1 illustrates a simple conceptual data model using this example. Each box represents a data group.

The data group name is generally a commonly understood business term. However, since different parts of the organization may have different definitions of the term, developing a common business definition for the data group is imperative to the process. If the model is to be used outside of the Information Systems group or as a communication tool among IS teams, it is best if the definition is developed by the business community.

Some organizations elect to define relationships between data groups. At this high level, these relationships represent business rules. For example, a customer may place one or many different orders, or a product may be supplied by one and only one vendor. These basic business rules are helpful in allowing the Information Systems team to understand the underlying business concepts that they must support.

Several approaches to conceptual data model documentation are possible within CASE tools. KnowledgeWare's Planning Workstation (PWS) provides a variety of objects that can be used to document data groupings. Entities can be used with or without relationships through the Entity Relationship Diagram. Data Collections can be defined to meet the requirements of the modeling project. For example, a data collection may represent a group of physical files or a database. Subject Areas are another option for documenting data groups. Subject Areas and Data Collections have the advantage of being able to be associated with entities and a subset of the entity diagram to be displayed for the grouping. This association allows the different groupings to occur, such as the grouping of detailed data groups (entities) into major categories (Subject Areas) or the identification of how current data (entities) map to planned data directions (Data Collections). Information Needs are yet another option for data group documentation. Many associations, or relationships, among these objects can be created and displayed in the Association Matrix. Subject Areas, Data Collections, and Information Needs can also be decomposed, or broken down into lower levels of detail, using the Decomposition Diagrammer tool.

For conceptual data modelers using only KnowledgeWare's Analysis Workstation (AWS), Entities and Subject Areas are

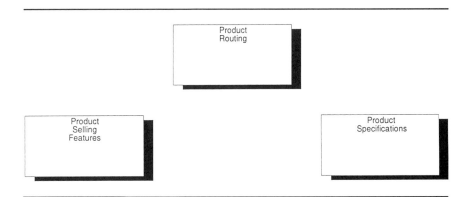

Figure 3.1.   Entity Relationship Diagrammer : conceptual data
model.

available. The Entity Relationship Diagram can be used to diagram entities and to identify the entities that occur in a subject
area. The Decomposition Diagrammer can be used to decompose
Subject Areas.

One possible implementation of all four objects could be to use
Subject Areas to represent high-level data groupings, such as Customer and Product. Entities could then represent more detailed
groupings, such as Customer Address and Product Specifications.
If the Subject Areas and Entities represent requirements, the
Data Collections could be used to document existing structures.
These structures could then be cross-referenced to the requirements using an Association Matrix to identify requirements that
are met by existing structures. Information Needs could then be
used to track the critical needs of the business. The Association
Matrix Diagrammer could then be used to link the information
needs to the Data Collections, illustrating how well existing structures meet critical needs, and to the Subject Areas, illustrating
how planned groupings would support those critical needs.

KnowledgeWare provides basic definitions of each one of these
objects and defines a specific set of predefined properties designed
to assist the planner in categorizing data groups. Some planning
methodologies also specify how specific objects, such as subject
areas, are to be used in a planning project. However, the conceptual data modeler is free to utilize this group of objects in the way

that provides the most benefit to the organization. The model manager must ensure that if this model is to be combined with other models, all objects are used in the same way or have unique naming standards to clearly identify the intent of the object.

Even if the diagramming tools are not utilized, a simple list of objects can also be effective with the CASE tool serving as the repository of definitions for those objects. KnowledgeWare allows the entry of definitions and comments for all object types. If relationships are not documented, it may be helpful to maintain a list of business rules, either within or outside of the CASE tool, to help document early requirements.

Logical Data Model

The logical data model is a more detailed version of the conceptual data model. It represents a more complete definition of the components of the data group. In many data analysis methodologies, the refined data groups are called entities. The data group CUSTOMER may become the entities CUSTOMER ADDRESS, CUSTOMER BUYING PROFILE, and CUSTOMER DISCOUNT. Specific data elements are identified and assigned to the entities as attributes of the entity. Customer Number, City Name, and State Code could be attributes of the CUSTOMER ADDRESS entity. Relationships are commonly defined between entities to represent business rules that relate data. A CUSTOMER DISCOUNT may apply to one or many different PRODUCTs, or it may apply to one and only one PRODUCT GROUP.

The entity and relationship information is usually illustrated in an entity-relationship diagram format, as shown in Figure 3.2. This format uses boxes to represent entities and lines to represent relationships between entities. The symbols on the relationships indicate the cardinalities of the relationships. As described in Chapter 2, cardinalities used in this diagram format identify how many occurrences of one entity exist for an occurrence of the other entity and whether the relationship is required or optional. In this diagram, a Product may be supplied by many vendors. A Product may exist without being supplied by a vendor. The specific format used to display the logical data model on this diagram is only one possible format.

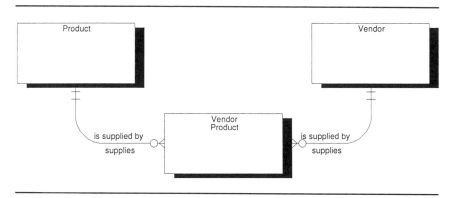

Figure 3.2.   Entity Relationship Diagrammer : logical data model.

Attributes are assigned to entities based on rules of normalization. These rules help define the primary key of an entity and ensure that all attributes within the entity are totally dependent on the primary key. For example, the VENDOR entity may be uniquely identified by the Vendor Number. The Vendor Name would be an attribute on the VENDOR entity since only one name exists for a specific Vendor Number. However, the Vendor Product Price would not be an attribute of VENDOR since price is specific to the combination of a Vendor and a Product. A new entity, VENDOR PRODUCT, with primary keys of Vendor Number and Product Number, would be required to support the Vendor Product Price attribute. This new entity is illustrated in Figure 3.2.

By applying the rules of normalization, experienced data analysts can design a set of entities and their associated attributes that correctly reflect the business requirements for data. It is important to note that technical database constraints are not introduced at this level. Instead the data analyst is focusing on capturing true business information without concern for the technical platform. This allows postponement of the platform selection until all requirements have been understood.

In a reverse engineering environment, this type of model allows true business information structures to be analyzed without the constraints of a specific database management system. A database model or a group of database models can be combined to a logical level by removing any aspects of the data design that are specific to the database management system. By using the same normalization techniques applied in new data analysis, a true representation of the data as it exists today is possible.

Relationships between entities further assist in the analysis of business requirements because they allow the visualization of linkages between data. Technically, relationships represent key-based dependencies between entities. The one-to-many relationship between the VENDOR entity and the VENDOR PRODUCT entity represents the fact that the primary key of VENDOR, Vendor Number, is a part of the VENDOR PRODUCT entity. Application designers can use this relationship to understand data navigation paths. Yet this relationship also documents critical business rules. From a business perspective, the relationship represents the fact that one VENDOR may offer several different PRODUCTs that are used by the organization.

CASE tools greatly assist in the development and maintenance of logical data models. Many data analysts have horror stories of data models with 25 or more entities that were drawn by hand. When a new relationship was identified, it was usually between entities on opposite sides of the hand-drawn diagram. Either the diagram was completely redrawn, or difficult-to-follow connector boxes were used. Although diagramming tools made the initial documentation easier, changes were just as difficult. Since CASE tools are specifically designed to support entity model development, movement of entities and changes in relationships are comparatively easy to accomplish. Models with over 100 entities are now feasible to develop and maintain.

CASE tools also facilitate the tracking of detailed attributes. Some allow the existence of keys to be implied by relationships, rather than duplicating attribute definitions in multiple places. This is especially helpful in a situation like Product Identifier, which may occur as a part of the key in a majority of entities in an application. Maintenance to this attribute can occur in a single place, the PRODUCT entity. Other such development aids include the establishment of data classes that allow data elements with similar properties, such as the same format, to be grouped together. For example, a PRICE class may be created and used by all price-related attributes. If the corporate definition for price expands, it can be changed in a single place.

The KnowledgeWare tool set allows the model developer to document logical entities and relationships through the Entity Relationship Diagrammer tool in the Analysis Workstation (AWS). Release 2.7 of this tool supports the majority of the logical data modeling concepts in the industry today, including supertypes and subtypes.

The attributes can then be specified for each entity on the Entity Type Description Diagram. An attribute or a group of attributes and relationships can be specified to be a unique key. Minimum and maximum cardinalities can be captured for the relationships and the attributes. Relationships can be used to document the existence of keys in one entity that are used as a part of a key in another entity.

Release 2.7 allows the definition of an Information Type. This documents the values that can apply to an attribute. For example, the attribute EMPLOYEE TYPE CODE may have a value of Exempt or Hourly. Information Types may be composed of other Information Types, such as a date composed of a month, day, and year. The Information Type Diagrammer has been designed specifically for this purpose. In prior releases, the Data Type was used to document this information at a more physical level.

Physical Data Model

The physical data model is the representation of the physical database that is implemented. Although it is likely to look similar to the logical data model, it has been modified to perform efficiently in the selected implementation environment. The physical data model includes data structures, which may be any physical implementation format including relational tables, hierarchical files, or even sequential files. Each of these data structures can contain specific data elements and, in the case of nonrelational structures, groupings of data elements.

Like the conceptual data model, the physical data model is not necessarily a diagram. It may be the physical file definition within a database management system or it may be a set of file layouts defined within a Code Generation CASE tool. Some tools do provide for the option of graphically representing the physical data model. The diagrams look similar to the logical data models, but physical data structure names have replaced the business terms used as entity names. The PRODUCT entity has become the PROD table. The VENDOR PRODUCT and VENDOR entities may have been combined into a single physical VPROD file. Relationships, if shown, represent actual paths that are available within the database (Figure 3.3).

KnowledgeWare's Design Workstation allows the documentation of physical data structures using data structure objects. In releases prior to 2.7, these include template data structures, which can be used in multiple structures; relations, which represent tables in relational databases; and files, which represent nondatabase structures. These structures can be grouped into database objects. Data Types define the format and type of the elements.

Release 2.7 dramatically changes the development and maintenance of physical models. A copy of the logical model is made, creating Catalog Entities, Catalog Attributes, and Catalog Relationships. These catalog objects can then be used to create physical structures including relational tables, segments for IMS, or global data records that are generic and can represent any structure. To add data elements that are not present in the logical model or to create data structures independent of a logical model, global or local data structures are used. Global structures can be used in other structures; local structures are specific to this structure. The format and type of element is defined by a Data Type that is based on the Information Type in the logical model.

The detail explained above can be developed, viewed, and modified in the Data Structure Diagram. Other diagrammers are available in the Design Workstation to see how data structures relate. Release 2.7 provides the Data Schema Diagrammer to illustrate the relationships between global data structures.

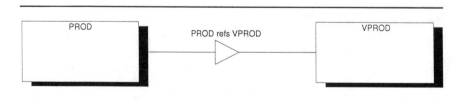

Figure 3.3.   Relational Schema Diagrammer : Vendor Product.

The Relational Schema Diagrammer illustrates the relationship between relational tables, while the Hierarchical Schema Diagrammer illustrates the relationship between hierarchical objects. The File Schema Diagrammer allows global records to be grouped into files. Diagrammers are also available to assist developers in defining the more technical aspects of database definition, such as Storage Groups and Tablespaces in DB2.

Business Data Models

Although physical data models represent actual computerized data structures, conceptual and logical data models do not necessarily represent actual or proposed computerized structures. These higher-level, business-oriented models may illustrate manual, paper files that are maintained by the business community. For example, files may be kept by the Human Resources department for recent applicants, applicants interviewed for the past year, and terminated employees. Data models can help the organization document these files and the information contained within them, providing an inventory of available information.

Within KnowledgeWare, this type of model could be documented in the Planning or Analysis Workstation. In the Planning Workstation, the entities, subject areas, information needs, and data collections could be utilized and associated to each other to fully document the types of information used by the organization. For example, a memo could be set up as a data collection that was cross-referenced to several entities, illustrating the types of information shown on the memo. Another alternative available through the Planning or Analysis Workstation is the use of the Entity Relationship Diagrammer to document the different types of information and their relationship. For example, if both Marketing and Finance track information about a Product, two entities could be established, one called PRODUCT MARKETING and the other called PRODUCT COST. Both of these could be defined as a part of a subject area called Product or could be related to another entity called PRODUCT that was defined as the base product information used by all departments, perhaps maintained by a centralized group.

USES OF DATA MODELS

Design of New Structures

Data models are commonly used to assist in the design of new data structures. The conceptual data model can serve to identify the need for new data structures. For example, it may document the need to track forecasting information that may not be recorded in a computerized fashion currently. The conceptual model may also identify required relationships between major groupings of information in the organization. In the forecasting example, the forecasting information may be required at a Product, Fiscal Week level.

Once the need for information and its relationship to other data is identified, the logical model can help detail business requirements for data. The definition of entities assists the organization in understanding precisely what is meant by commonly used terms. The EMPLOYEE entity from a payroll perspective may mean an individual who is currently being paid through the payroll system. However, the Human Resources department may view an employee as anyone who has ever signed a hiring agreement with the firm, including new employees who have not yet reported for work and terminated employees who are no longer being paid. It is critical that the two groups resolve the discrepancy in terminology to be able to share a common data structure in the future.

The definition of relationships, especially cardinalities, can also serve to resolve potential conflicts in future data structure design. Using the employee example, if current business rules state that an employee can be in only one job at a time, supporting data structures and corresponding logic will be developed. A pay rate could be assigned to a job and applied to all employees in the job. However, if it is known that employees may be in multiple jobs at the same time, a different set of data structures and logic are required. For example, to pay an employee, a primary job may be identified for pay purposes or pay rates may be defined for the employee independent of the job.

The definition of attributes reconciles terminology conflicts at a detailed level. Defining the data elements required and correctly assigning them to an entity requires strong communication about how the business operates. Is an employee's pay rate based on his or her job, or is a flat pay rate assigned to the employee? Attribute definition often involves the assigning of lengths and formats, which will be critical to the final data structure design. Business issues, such as the maximum number of employees who will potentially be tracked, must be considered.

Once the logical data model is complete, the physical data model can be defined. In this logical to physical translation process, the data modeler applies technical knowledge of the database platform. For example, if sequential files are selected, several entities may be combined into a single data structure to improve processing efficiency. If a relational database is the target environment, the entities may be translated almost one for one into tables.

Analyze Relationships Between Existing Data Structures

As more tools support some form of reverse engineering, data models are increasingly used to analyze relationships between existing data structures. Few organizations have had the luxury of developing integrated databases from scratch. Most organizations have gradually accumulated a collection of data structures using multiple technical platforms. In addition, many individuals have likely participated in the development of those structures. It is rare to find a single individual who is aware of all of the structures and how they relate to each other.

By creating a model of critical data structures and their relationships, the organization can learn a great deal about its data for the purposes of both new applications development and applications maintenance. If the business community is actively utilizing information using its own tool set, it can also benefit by understanding the relationships between commonly used data.

For analytical purposes, the logical data model is the most commonly used type of data model. Reverse engineering creates a physical data model from existing documentation, such as file layouts. A logical model is then created from the physical model. Although some tools can automate this process to some degree, the key-based relationships generally must be added or refined manually. The end result is a representation of the critical entities and their relationships. Attributes may also be documented.

An example of this type of model is a product database. Product information is generally critical to manufacturing and sales-oriented firms. Data structures containing product information may reside on multiple platforms, supporting multiple applications. An inventory file may contain product inventory standards; a table maintenance file may contain the product description for sales purposes; a manufacturing file may contain the product specifications for production. All this information may logically be represented in one entity called PRODUCT. A product may have many prices, represented by a one-to-many relationship to a PRICE entity. The PRICE entity may represent multiple price files, each one specific to a grouping of customers (see Figure 3.4).

In current releases, KnowledgeWare does not provide facilities to completely reverse-engineer data. The "reengineer" facility available within Encyclopedia Services will use data definitions, such as a record layout in COBOL data definition format, to create generic physical data structures. Utilities that will take this information and convert it to entity relationship diagrams in the Analysis Workstation are available through other vendors.

Analyze Business Information

Although we frequently think of data models in terms of computerized data structures, data models may also represent documents, forms, and files that are maintained on paper media by the firm. By depicting these types of information in a data model, the firm can identify underlying relationships between existing documents and determine possible improvements.

The Human Resources department may keep a file of employee address forms to use for verifying addresses for mailing purposes. The Payroll department may also keep a copy of the forms to use as backup documentation for the changes made to the payroll system. This duplication of manual files could possibly be replaced by a single file, accessible to both departments. Or perhaps the Human Resources department could further automate its mailing process by using the updated addresses maintained by the Payroll department. The model could help identify

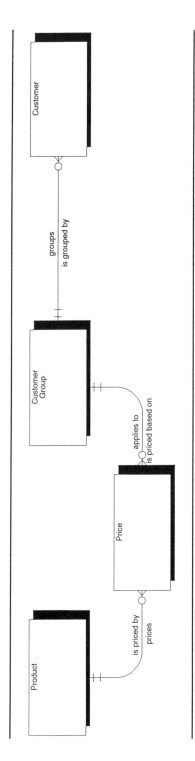

Figure 3.4. Entity Relationship Diagrammer : Product database.

this duplication of files and the existence of computerized files to assist the departments in analyzing a potential efficiency and storage improvement.

Logical or conceptual data models are used more frequently to represent business information. Attributes may be defined to document the specific pieces of business data that are used. In this type of model, the emphasis is not on developing a normalized model with very detailed attributes, but rather on representing existing information as the business views it. Entities and relationships tend to be the best documentation mechanism.

DATA MODELS IN THE LIFE CYCLE

Planning

Data models can be deliverables from planning activities. At this phase in the life cycle, conceptual data models are generally produced. Planning data models can serve two distinct purposes. A future data model documents major data areas that will be of interest to the organization in the future. If an assessment of existing data structures is performed during the planning phase, a model of current data areas or collections may be documented.

Based on the methodology in use at the organization, the planning data model may be either corporate-wide or for a specific project. Corporate-wide, or enterprise, data models are generally developed during a strategic systems planning project. This model serves as the foundation for the development of a strategic data plan by identifying critical data areas for the future. If planning is considered the first phase of an information systems project, the model will focus on identifying major groupings of data for a specific area of the business. This model will be considered by later phases of the project.

Planning data models may be developed by the Information Systems staff, a planning group, the Data Administration staff, or a team composed of Information Systems and business representatives. Since conceptual models do not necessarily conform to standard data model convention, such as full normalization, business and senior Information Systems management can easily develop these models. The critical result should be the identification of future business directions that should be considered in future data design. Therefore, the model could be as simple as a list of major data groupings, with a description of how they will be used in the future. More complex models could be developed, with entities and relationships, if an experienced data analyst is available to assist in the process.

Situations to look for in planning data models include specific areas where data is not meeting user needs and areas where the business will change existing business rules in the future. For example, the business may be supplementing computerized files with its own set of PC based spreadsheets to capture additional information that could easily be integrated into existing data structures. Critical business changes may include a restructure of the pricing scheme from price based on quantity purchased to price based on customer group. If separate structures and systems are maintained for existing channels of distribution, the addition of a new wholesale distribution channel may require extensive rework to existing structures. A business emphasis on a centralized budgeting function may yield the definition of a new budget data group, which may currently be represented by multiple budget files maintained by separate systems and departments.

Analysis

Logical data models are developed during the analysis phase of a project. If a planning data model is available, developing the analysis data model is the further definition of that model. In the absence of the planning data model, the creation of the initial analysis data model may involve research into business directions and existing data that supports the area. In both cases, reverse engineering of existing data structures may be required to identify existing files to be redesigned or used as integration points.

Once an initial logical data model is defined, the project team refines the model to identify entities, attributes, and relationships. The goal at this phase is to document all business data requirements and data-related business rules, irrespective of the planned physical implementation. Knowledgeable representatives of the business community and the Information Systems staff are critical to this process.

Either as the model is being built or after the first cut of business definitions, rules, and requirements have been documented, an experienced data analyst should ensure that the model is properly normalized. This process will likely require business representatives to answer questions about data dependencies.

Design

With the final, normalized logical data model in place, the design team can apply its technical knowledge to define an efficient set of physical structures. In a database environment, Database Administration will play a critical role in this physical data model design. The physical data model will likely change throughout this phase as more is discovered about access of the data in the application. At this phase, there is a careful balance between creating efficient structures for the specific application and developing flexible structures that can be used across applications.

The physical data model itself may be documented in a CASE tool, or it may reside within the dictionary or catalog of the database management system. In either situation, tools are available that can help depict a graphical picture of the database designed.

If the logical data model is to be maintained permanently, all changes to the physical data model should first be analyzed to see if changes are required in the logical data model. Logical data model impacts include new or changed business rules, requirements, or definitions. For example, if an organization moves to an environment where a product can now be produced at multiple plants, the logical data model may need to be changed to represent a one-to-many relationship between the product entity and the plant entity. However, if the product and product specification entities were consolidated into one physical structure with multiple specifications available for the product, a one-to-many relationship between a product entity and a product specification entity would remain untouched since the business rules had not changed.

Construction/Implementation

The physical data model is refined during this stage of project development. Hopefully, the change rate has slowed since the design phase and the model is simply being fine tuned. A more detailed physical data model may be developed at this point as more information is gathered about structure volumes and accesses.

Maintenance

In the maintenance phase, it is possible that the conceptual, logical, and physical data models could require maintenance. Major shifts in business directions may necessitate a change to the conceptual model, while a minor change in the volume of a physical data structure may cause an update to the physical data model. Correct maintenance of all data models requires careful analysis of the impact of a change on all three models and completing all required maintenance.

Packaged Software Implementation

Data models can play an important role in assisting software package implementation and support teams. Physical data models can help the team understand the technical data aspects of the system and can generally be developed easily from documentation provided by the vendor. Logical data models can provide a means of explaining available information to the individuals who will actually use the package and its information on a daily basis. They can also be a mechanism for developing integration points with existing logical and physical data structures. However, few vendors today deliver logical data models. Some reverse engineering tools may be able to create initial logical data models from physical models, but a great deal of work, including renaming to business terms, will still be required.

REQUIREMENTS FOR DATA MODEL MAINTENANCE

Maintaining Physical Data Models

In CASE tools that support code generation, active maintenance of the physical data model used by the generator is a requirement if specifications, rather than generated source code, are to be maintained. But in other environments, the requirements for physical data model maintenance are not as clearly defined.

Even in environments where code generation is not yet in use, active maintenance of the physical data model can prove beneficial. The system maintenance staff can use the diagram to assist in analyzing proposed changes and problem areas. Major enhancement projects can use the model as a starting point for developing new structures and modifying existing ones. Users of data query facilities and languages can use the diagrams to plan data access and usage. Teams developing systems that will integrate with the physical structures can find the diagram helpful in their design process.

Maintaining the physical data model is a relatively simple task, since it is easy to verify the accuracy of the model by comparing the model directly to actual file definitions. Many CASE tools offer facilities to build physical data structures from actual file definitions, making it easy to update structures with changes.

The relational translation facility within KnowledgeWare allows the automatic generation of a database design with all required objects from the logical data requirements represented in the entity model. This information can then be maintained when changes occur to the physical model. If the logical model is changed, the physical model can be manually changed or regenerated. KnowledgeWare also provides a reverse engineering facility for data described earlier in this chapter that creates KnowledgeWare objects from file definitions and selected types of database definitions. By using this facility, the model manager can quickly populate the Design Workstation with accurate representation of existing physical structures.

The model manager may elect to take one of two approaches to actual maintenance of the physical model. The distinction between the two approaches is based on the method of physical data design. If the CASE tool itself is used to support data design work, the change would occur directly within the tool and then be transferred to the source of physical file definition, such as the database management system. If the database developers do not use the organization's CASE tools or if they work with a set of tools that is independent of the standard models supported by model management, the change may first occur to the physical file definition and then be made to the model in the CASE tool.

For example, the model manager may be responsible for all

models developed using KnowledgeWare CASE tools. The Database administration team may use Bachman CASE tools to refine the database design. The model manager must then determine how to ensure that the KnowledgeWare model matches the Bachman model. If code is actually generated from the model in the KnowledgeWare tool, it is even more critical that these models be identical. If a link is provided between database design models in the two tools, it could be used periodically to update the KnowledgeWare models from the Bachman models. If such an automated link is not available, the model manager may be required to update the KnowledgeWare models manually to match the Bachman models. A standard change control procedure in which the Database Administration team informs model management of changes to the physical database model will help determine the timing of the manual or automated updates.

Maintaining Logical Data Models

The maintenance of logical data models is not as easy as physical data models. The primary reason is the difficulty in ensuring that the logical model is accurate. Since the physical data implementation may not exactly match the logical design, the data analyst must understand the valid differences between the two to accurately maintain the model. The integrity of the model is also constantly in question. The logical model should represent business requirements. A change to the logical model should therefore represent a change in the business requirements. The data analyst must identify that a physical data model change represents a business requirements change and therefore necessitates a logical data model change.

However, those organizations that elect to maintain their logical data models can achieve several distinct benefits. These models can assist in the communications process between the business community and Information Services. They use business terms and reflect business requirements and therefore are much easier to use as a starting point for analyzing changes or problems directly with the business. For new development projects, enhancements and additions to the data model can be analyzed first at the logical level, ensuring that the resulting physical structures reflect true business requirements. Data query design by the business is also better facilitated by the logical, rather than the physical, model.

Logical data model managers using the KnowledgeWare tool rely heavily on their knowledge of the names and definitions of entities to ensure that logical models are accurately maintained. Often this also involves knowledge of the business. For example, one analyst may call an entity Product, while another uses the term Item. The model manager must know the two are the same to accurately maintain the model. Standard naming conventions, such as attribute names being identical to physical data element names, can help somewhat in the model maintenance process, but most of the checking will be manual. Luckily, the tool will ensure that logical models that are combined conform to basic modeling conventions used by the tool. Therefore, the model manager can focus on the business, rather than the technical, aspects of model verification.

Care should be taken in the use of reverse engineering tools provided by other vendors to maintain the logical data model from the physical database design. Many tools support this type of reverse engineering by matching identical primary key data element names to identify relationships. Although this may appear to create the correct relationships, in certain circumstances it may give inaccurate results. The primary problem is a lack of organization-wide data element naming standards. Few tools can recognize that Product Number and Item Identifier represent the same logical data element.

Assumptions made about data design further complicate accurate logical model creation. Suppose the Purchased Product Table has Product Number as its primary key and the Manufactured Item Table also has Product Number as its primary key. Most tools will either create two entities and add a one-to-one relationship between them or will combine the two tables into one logical entity. If a product is either a purchased product or a manufactured item, the tool would have been incorrect using either approach. Therefore, if an automated reverse engineering tool is used to create a logical data model from a physical data model, the results should be carefully reviewed and modified to reflect the business and the data that supports it accurately.

Maintenance of the Conceptual Data Model

The conceptual data model is likely the most difficult to maintain. Due to its high level of abstraction, it generally bears little resemblance to the physical data model. Therefore, changes to the physical model are difficult to incorporate correctly into the conceptual model.

Most organizations that maintain the conceptual model do so as a part of a planning process that requires the maintenance of the planning data model. During planning projects, it is easier to identify major changes to business directions and the corresponding impact on data design.

The decision to maintain the conceptual data model should be based on the actual use of the model in the organization. If the model is the basis for an organization or business-area data strategy, annual updates in conjunction with the business planning process would be beneficial so that the data strategy could be updated accordingly. If the model is used to train new individuals within the business and Information Systems groups about data within the organization, its maintenance could also be critical. However, for organizations that simply use the conceptual data model as a starting point for logical data model development, maintenance of the conceptual model may provide little, if any, benefit.

Managers of conceptual models using KnowledgeWare face many of the same issues as logical model managers. However, because the tool offers many options in the documentation of conceptual models, the model manager must also ensure that any organization-specific requirements are met. For example, if all databases are to be documented as Data Collections, the model manager must develop a way to ensure that this is accomplished. It may be through a report that compares a list of physical databases to a list of data collections in KnowledgeWare or through manual checking at set periods of time, perhaps monthly. Standard procedures that ensure that the conceptual model manager is informed of all additions, deletions, and renames of databases are most effective in ensuring the accuracy of such a model.

KnowledgeWare's Release 2.7 provides new features in the Planning Workstation that facilitate this type of model management. Associations can be made between physical items maintained in the Design Workstation, such as relational databases, and conceptual items, such as data collections or subject areas. When a new physical item is added, required changes to the conceptual model could be identified by reviewing an Association Reporting Matrix for relational databases and subject areas. This feature is available for traceable association, or indirect relationships between objects. In this example, a subject area contains entities that are related to catalog entities. The catalog entities are referenced by relations, which are contained within relational databases. These complex association references can be created through Object Lists and then referenced repeatedly through the Association Reporting Matrix.

Linkage of Conceptual, Logical, and Physical Data Models

For organizations that elect to develop conceptual, logical, and physical data models, there is generally a progressive relationship between the three. The logical model is a more detailed version of the conceptual model. The physical model is the logical model modified for technical efficiency. Since these models were originally linked in the development process, the link may be continued through maintenance.

In integrated CASE tool environments, where a single vendor's tools are used throughout the life cycle, the linkage may be built into the tool. The data group may be associated with all the entities that implement it logically. Attributes may be linked to the specific data elements that are implemented physically. In multiple CASE tool environments, vendors may work together to provide a sort of linkage or the organization can use comments to document linkages.

The advantage to maintaining linkages is the ability to track and implement changes in all three models. If an attribute is added to an entity, the physical structures that are linked to the entity can be analyzed to determine the correct position of the resulting data element. If a data element format changes, the related attribute format can also be modified. If the definition of a data group is changed, all entities that are a part of the data group can be analyzed for possible changes. Without linkages, managing change to all three models would be difficult.

KnowledgeWare users can easily link logical and physical data objects through the use of ties prior to Release 2.7. These ties track relationships between a group of data elements and an entity, a specific data element and an attribute, and one or more data elements and a relationship. These can be generated automatically by the relational translation facility, which creates the physical model from the logical model and can then be maintained manually as the physical design changes. If major changes occur to the logical model, a completely new physical model can be generated to replace the old physical model. Portions of the model can be regenerated, but manual effort is required to link the old and new sections of the physical data model correctly.

Release 2.7 uses the concept of catalog entities, attributes, and relationships to create the linkage between the logical and physical models. Fundamentally, the catalog entity, attribute, and relationship is an object that represents the same information as the tie relationship. Since the linkage is now in the form of an object, it is easier to reference and manage through tools like the Object List.

The catalog entity model also introduces a new feature within the KnowledgeWare tool set that allows changes and deletions in the logical model to be propagated easily into the physical model. Prior to Release 2.7, the physical data model could be recreated from the logical model, but changes such as attribute renames and attribute additions could not be incorporated through an automatic facility. Under 2.7, a tool is available to create the catalog data model, applying updates or deletions. Once the new catalog data model has been created, a new physical data model can be generated. The changes only apply to catalog attributes that are used within the physical data structure. Any references to global or local data structures independent of the catalog attribute are retained. Although more objects must be maintained in this approach with the addition of the three new catalog objects, the ease of physical data model maintenance greatly enhances the model manager's productivity.

There is no single approach to linking logical and conceptual data models in the tool. Possible techniques include using Subject Areas to document conceptual data objects and then grouping Entities into those Subject Areas and using Data Collections to document conceptual objects and using the Association Matrix to cross-reference logical Entities to Data Collections.

Linkage of Planning and Current Data Models

If the conceptual or logical data model is developed as a part of a planning effort, the model may be distinct from actual systems project data models, which depict current data. By linking the current data model to the future data model, required changes and additions to current data can be easily identified.

However, linking these two models may not be a simple task. Most CASE tools support the progressive approach to model development but do not provide clear means of connecting two models at the same level. Associations could possibly be defined between data groups or entities, if supported by the tool. Comments areas or external cross-reference files are possibilities.

If the tool does not readily provide for current and future model linkages, the organization should carefully evaluate the true benefit before deciding to maintain the linkage long-term. If the planning data model plays a major role in directing applications development and data development activities, up-to-date knowledge of how well current data is supporting future directions may be critical. However, if the linkage is developed at a high, conceptual data model level and is only used periodically to plan annual activities, resources may be better allocated to rebuilding the linkage once a year as required.

The KnowledgeWare tool does not automatically provide for the linkage of future and current models. However, several manual techniques can prove successful. One is to prefix all future or current objects with a standard prefix, such as F- for future objects. This allows the current and future version of the Employee entity to exist in the same model and to be easily connected by the name. Another option is to use different objects that can be cross-referenced in a matrix, such as Entities for future data objects and Data Collections for current data objects. If detailed tracking is not required, the current and future objects could both be assigned to the same subject area. This would provide a current and future view of a set of data.

Tracking Project Data Usage

The most difficult task of data model maintenance is tracking data objects that are in use by multiple projects. Although this task is a challenge for all types of models, it is especially complex for data models in an integrated data environment. Central model areas, such as Product-related data models in a manufacturing environment, could be modified by a number of projects that are underway at a given point in time. Model managers must be aware of project implementation timetables and ensure that all projects that will be implemented after a change takes effect have knowledge of the change and correctly incorporate it into their project models.

Versioning can help accomplish this task. Although only a limited number of CASE tools officially provide versioning support, separate repositories of models can be implemented. This is relatively easy if each project team maintains its own set of models in a separate repository, such as on a workstation or file server. In environments where establishing separate copies of model information is not feasible, such as a mainframe CASE tool environment with limited storage space, the common model components might be named separately for each version to keep changes distinct. Some centralized group, such as Data Administration, could then ensure that all model changes are incorporated into the correct project specific models.

INFORMATION MODELS FOR DATA MODELING OBJECTS

The information model for data-related objects will be based on the type of data models the organization develops and how those models are linked, both initially and in maintenance. Although the exact object names may differ based on the CASE tool in use, a fully integrated, linked model may look like Figure 3.5. In this example, a Data Group may be implemented by many entities. An entity can have many attributes. An entity can be related to another entity

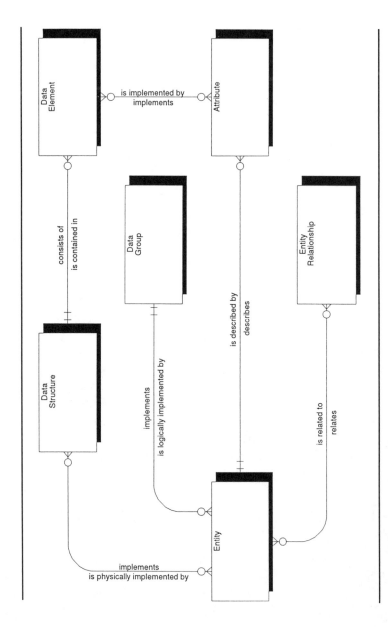

Figure 3.5. Entity Relationship Diagrammer : data information model.

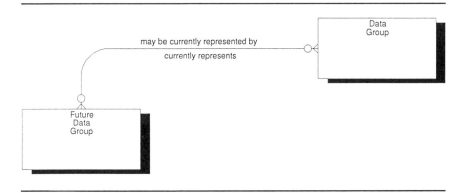

Figure 3.6.   Entity Relationship Diagrammer : future and current Data Groups.

through a relationship. A data structure may implement several entities, in the case of entities combined into a single file for efficiency reasons. An entity may be implemented by multiple data structures. A similar relationship holds for data elements and attributes. These relationships help the model managers to understand the integrity requirements of model maintenance.

This basic model can be tailored to an organization's environment. If one of the models is not developed or maintained, the associated objects would not appear. If the model linkages are not maintained, the relationships would not appear since they are not requirements for an object to exist. Data element groups may be added at a physical level if they are a part of the physical data model.

In environments where the current and future data models are linked, additional objects and/or relationships would be added to the model to depict the linkage. For example, if current data groups are linked to future data groups and no future logical or physical data groupings are tracked, except at a project maintenance level, a new object may be added for Future Data Groups and a relationship between Data Groups, now representing current data groups, and Future Data Groups would be added (Figure 3.6).

Developing a Customized Data Information Model

Since each organization will approach data modeling in a slightly different manner, based on the methodology, CASE tools, and data model goals in place, each organization will have its own unique data information model. The following questions are designed to assist the organization in developing an initial data information model. After this initial model is complete, the organization will need to identify which objects and relationships are required, which are optional, and which properties apply to each object.

1. Will the conceptual data model be maintained?

If so, add an entity for each object used to store conceptual data. Examples are Subject Areas, Data Classes, Entities, and Data Groups.

2. What are the relationships between these conceptual data objects?

Add relationship lines indicating relationships between conceptual objects. For example, if a Subject Area contains many Entities, draw a one-to-many relationship line between Entities and Subject Areas. If an Entity can appear in many Subject Areas, change the relationship to a many-to-many relationship.

3. Will the logical data model be maintained?

If so, add an entity for each object used to store logical data. Examples are Entities, Attributes, and Entity Relationships. Even though Entity Relationships appear to be only linkages between entities, most methodologies track relationship names and cardinalities. If this is the case, the Entity Relationship should be an object.

4. What are the relationships between logical data objects?

Add relationship lines indicating relationships between logical objects. For example, if an entity contains many attributes, draw a one-to-many relationship between entities and attributes. If an attribute can describe multiple entities, change the relationship to a many-to-many.

If an entity can participate in multiple-entity relationships, draw a one-to-many relationship between Entity and Relationship. If an Entity Relationship can have more than one entity (most do relate at least two entities), change the relationship to a many-to-many relationship. For organizations that do not establish an entity relationship object, this type of relationship can simply be recursive for the entity object, which means the relationship goes both into and out of the entity object.

5. Will the physical data model be maintained?

If so, add an entity for each object used to store physical data. Examples are Data Structures, Data Elements, Files, Fields, Tables, and Columns. In identifying these objects, it is helpful to consider objects that are tracked by tools other than traditional CASE tools such as source management packages.

6. What are the relationships between physical data objects?

Most models will have some sort of hierarchy. For example, a file may contain many fields, and a field may be used in many files. To indicate this, draw a many-to-many relationship between file and field.

In these physical objects, the definition of the objects is critical. Does a data structure represent a specific file or table? If so, it may have a one-to-one relationship with a file and/or table. Can a data structure represent a group of data elements? If so, a file may contain many data structures. Can a data structure contain a data structure? If so, a recursive relationship is needed for data structure.

7. Is there a need to identify which logical entities comprise a conceptual data group?

If so, a one-to-many relationship should be added between the appropriate conceptual data object and the entity. If any entity can be contained in multiple occurrences of the conceptual data object, the relationship should be a many-to-many relationship.

8. *Is there a need to compare the logical model to its physical implementation?*

If so, a relationship is needed to help track the physical version of the logical model. In many cases, this relationship could be a many-to-many relationship between the entity and a physical data object, such as a data structure, a file, or a table. Due to denormalization, it is not likely that this relationship will be one-to-many in either direction.

9. *Is there a need to compare logical attributes to their physical implementation?*

If the organization needs to track at this finite level of detail, the relationship between the entity and the physical data object may be replaced by a relationship between an attribute and a data element. Since attributes are usually linked to entities and data elements to a physical data object, the relationship identified in question 8 would be redundant.

10. *Will details be maintained about logical attributes as well as physical data elements?*

If a linkage was identified in question 9, the organization should carefully evaluate the properties of attributes and data elements. Should formats be defined for both? Should definitions be defined for both? The deciding factor should be whether the format, definition, or other duplicate property can differ at the physical level. If so, the property needs to be tracked at both levels. Other areas of the model that are linked should also be evaluated for similar redundancies of detailed properties.

The approach outlined through these questions creates a basic information model, such as that shown in Figure 3.5. It is only one possible approach to information model development. An experienced data analyst in the organization can customize these questions and the resulting instructions to match the data analysis techniques in use by the organization. In this approach, no attempt was made to develop a fully normalized data model since the purpose was to identify basic business requirements. If the organization wishes to use the resulting model to build a repository structure, additional refinement may be required.

ACTIVITY MODELS FOR DATA MODEL MANAGEMENT

The activity model for data model management illustrates the major tasks to be performed in managing data objects and their linkages. A sample activity model is displayed in Figure 3.7. This model divides activities into major groups based on the types of functions the model manager performs. Identifying objects, linkages, and associated standards is viewed as one major function. Providing all necessary groups with access to the models is a second. The third functional grouping includes major tasks required to ensure the validity of the models.

Figure 3.8 illustrates how the information model is used by one task, reconciling redundant objects. This sample shows that different objects may have different criteria for redundancy identification. For attributes and data elements, the model manager may consider the name, format, and definition. For relationships, the components of the relationship may be critical. By documenting this type of detail in the activity model, the requirements and procedures of model management can be detailed.

Developing a Customized Data Activity Model

Just as each organization will have its own information model, it will also have its own activity model. The structure of the activity model will likely differ based on the way in which the organization assigns responsibility for model management activities. The specific tasks will also differ since each organization will have different priorities as well as different objects to be managed. The following questions have been designed to assist the organization in developing an initial data activity model. The emphasis at this stage should be on identifying the required tasks. In later chapters, options for organizing the model will be discussed.

1. Who will use the models?

The audience of the models determines what types of accesses need to be provided by the model management team. If the mod-

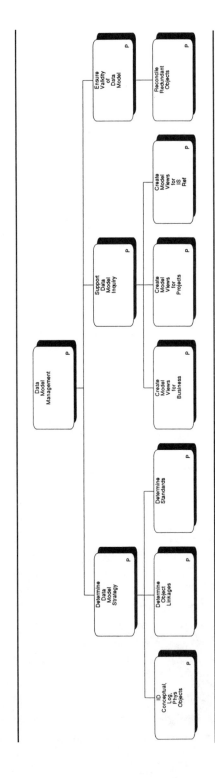

Figure 3.7. Decomposition Diagrammer : data model management.

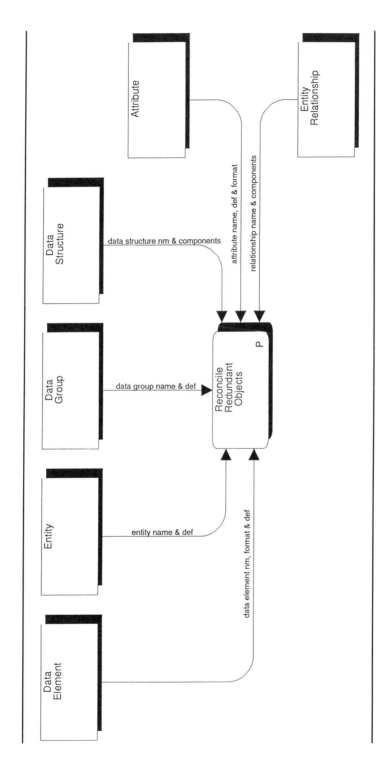

Figure 3.8. Data Flow Diagrammer : ensuring validity of data model.

els are only used by the Information Systems group in conjunction with project activities, the model management tasks may be based around the organization's project development life cycle. However, if the models are needed for basic inquiry by the business or the Information Systems staff, more tasks may be required to make these models easily available.

2. When will they need access to the models?

If immediate access is required at any time, the model manager needs to provide facilities for user access of models. If the access is known in advance, the model manager can personally process requests for models and provide manual control of the models. By identifying the different situations when access will be required, the model manager can better define detailed procedures that meet the needs of the model users.

3. How will conceptual and logical models be verified?

The activities required to ensure valid models are critical to model management. It is important that mechanisms are established to ensure that the models are valid. With conceptual and logical data models, these mechanisms could include business review groups, existing database design, and information requirements uncovered by new projects.

4. How will physical models be verified?

Most organizations utilize source management or database management software that tracks details of physical data structures. This software can provide important input into the verification of physical models. An automated facility is optimal, but a manual procedure of comparing the contents of the repository to the source or database management software is feasible.

These are some of the major issues to be evaluated in developing the activity model. Each organization will identify activities specific to data model management as it gains experience in model development, usage, and management.

4

Process Model
Management

TYPES OF PROCESS MODELS

Process models are representations of the functions and activities of the business or a system that supports the business. Like data models, process models can be in diagram or textual form. They are commonly used to analyze current activities and provide the basis for process improvement.

Business Process Model

A business process model is a representation of the business activities that occur within the organization. This model may be developed for the entire organization, illustrating at a high level the major functions of the business, or at a more detailed level, showing the specific activities performed by a group. These business process models can be valuable in documenting current business functions. This documentation not only helps Information Systems groups understand the business functions they support, but can also help to educate the business on the actual activities that take place.

    The high-level conceptual business process model is similar to the conceptual data model. It is used for planning purposes by both Information Systems and the entire organization to document the future emphases of the firm. Often a model at this level looks very similar to an organizational chart, with major areas such as Financial Management, Manufacturing, and Marketing. However, in some cases this model can illustrate how the business could be better organized to meet future goals. For example, the model may show that the Marketing area is supporting two distinct functions, Sales and Order Processing. As a result of the model, Order Processing may be identified as its own area, distinct from the Sales function, and a new high-level department may be established to handle this vital function.

A more detailed model can help analyze specific activities within the organization. These models can focus on one department, such as Forecasting, or may encompass several departments, such as a Sales Reporting Analysis project. As with the higher-level models, the more detailed models can help design organizational changes by highlighting areas of redundancy of effort or unnecessary activities.

A decomposition diagram format is most commonly used for business process analysis (Figure 4.1). The sample shows the business view of processing an order. The major components include receiving the order, processing it, preparing the invoice, and sending the order to the Distribution group. This business process model includes both automated and manual processes and uses business terminology.

By allowing a process to be shown in increasingly lower levels of detail, the decomposition diagram format provides both a high-level summary and a detailed representation. A flowchart is another possible representation of a process model. It has the advantage of illustrating activity sequence and dependencies but is at a fixed level of detail. A simple list of major functions, perhaps in outline form to achieve some of the benefits of summary and detailed information, could also be developed as a process model.

Many CASE tools that support planning and analysis activities include process diagrammers. These tools are specifically designed to support the decomposition or flowchart process and therefore make process models easy to develop and maintain. As CASE tools increase in use, the popularity of process modeling is growing, since developing and maintaining an accurate model is finally realistic.

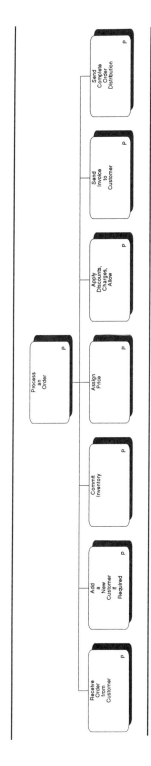

Figure 4.1. Decomposition Diagrammer : Process an Order.

KnowledgeWare supports process modeling through the use of process and function objects. A decomposition diagrammer can be used to decompose a function into processes or a process into subprocesses. Definitions and comments can be used to document specific business details. Processes can also be cross-referenced to planning objects, such as information needs.

Modeling Information System Processes

The process decomposition diagram can also be used to document the processes to be performed in an information system. For online functions, a higher-level process may represent a menu, while the lower-level processes are the screens that are available from the menu. For batch functions, the individual programs that are used in job steps may be grouped together by a process that represents a job.

The objects contained in the information system process model are representations of the menus, screens, reports, and batch processes that will compose the application. Based on the audience for the model, these will either be named based on organizational standards for screens, reports, and programs, or they may be named based on actual business activities so that the business can interpret the model.

A sample information system process model is shown in Figure 4.2. This model represents the same process shown in Figure 4.1, but it has been modified to represent the order processing information system. Four major screens are required to complete the business process. A process such as Product Selection may support several different business processes, including price selection and inventory commitment.

Individual CASE tools may store these as the same type of object or may establish special objects for each type of application component. Some tools provide a generic Process object where all this information can be stored. Naming standards or prefixes can be used to distinguish between the different types of processes. Other tools may provide objects such as logical screens, logical reports, and logical programs that represent the requirement for a physical object but do not include the detailed specifications or layouts.

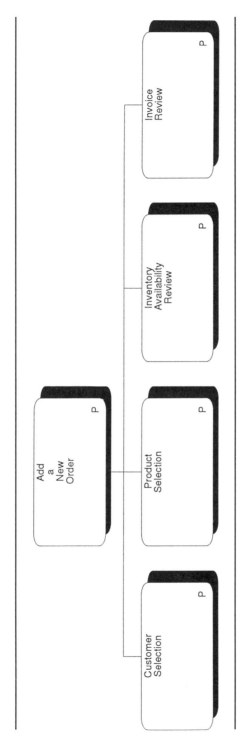

Figure 4.2. Decomposition Diagrammer : Add a New Order.

73

A user of KnowledgeWare's tool set has two options for documenting the system process model. One alternative is to use processes within the Analysis Workstation to document the system structure. Prefixes or Suffixes could be used to identify whether an object is a screen, report, program, or menu. If the Design Workstation is used, the structure could be documented using module objects. Screens and Reports could be represented by modules or by screen objects. Release 2.7 allows the use of report objects in addition to screen objects.

A special type of decomposition diagram is a structure chart. Some tools allow the use of a structure chart to document the system components, as explained above. Other tools use a structure chart to diagram the specific components of a program. In either case, the structure chart illustrates the interaction of system components.

Figure 4.3 illustrates a structure chart for a program. This would be the Product Selection program identified in Figure 4.2. The major logic sections are displayed on this diagram. Two major sections are displaying the product list itself and processing selected products. For selected products, detailed processing, such as price assignment, occurs. This type of diagram helps the developer design the flow of a program.

The objects contained in a traditional structure chart are the programs or the modules used as a part of the program. These are generally named based on organization-specific program-, routine-, and paragraph-naming standards.

KnowledgeWare's structure chart diagrammer graphically illustrates the calling structure of a program or a system itself. The level of detail depends on what modules are established by the developer. The concept is similar to a decomposition diagrammer, with the addition of details about the type of call that is planned. The tool automatically makes this information available to the specification developer and ensures that the diagram and specification coincide. For example, if the structure chart shows Program 1 calling Subroutine 1, the tool adds a Call Command to Subroutine 1 in the specification for Program 1. The specification is accessible through the Action Diagram tool.

Some CASE tools treat screen and report layouts and program specifications as types of process models. Since an increas-

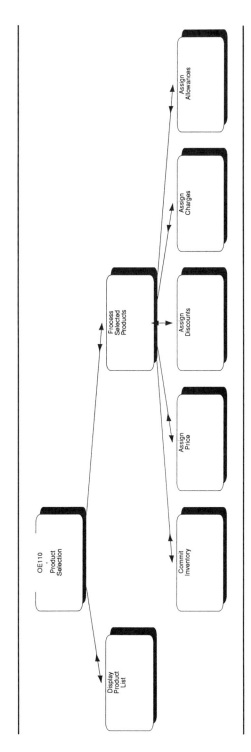

Figure 4.3.   Structure Chart Diagrammer : Module OE110 : Product Selection.

ing number of tools, including KnowledgeWare, use these models to help link processes and data, they will be discussed as linkage objects in Chapter 5.

Planning Process Models

A special type of process model can be developed during the planning phase of projects. Usually this model is the conceptual business process model. However, it may also include some aspects of an information system process model.

In addition to capturing the basic business functions and processes as described in the conceptual business process model, the planning team could also track other details about the organization. KnowledgeWare provides special objects such as goals, critical success factors, and information needs to facilitate complete documentation of the business direction. These objects complement the process model by providing the rationale for the model.

In addition to documenting directions, models can also be produced that document, at a high level, the major applications in place in the organization. Projects, both current and planned, could also be identified. These two dimensions could then be compared to the process model to identify how current and planned systems are used by the organization.

In addition to the process and function objects, KnowledgeWare's Planning Workstation supports the documentation of business processes through a series of planning objects, including Goals, Critical Success Factors, and Information Needs. A variety of matrices are available to document the relationships between these planning objects. Due to the large number of combinations available, model managers using KnowledgeWare need to identify the specific planning objects and matrices that provide the highest benefit to the organization and will be maintained in the long run.

USES OF PROCESS MODELS

Design New Information Systems

Business process models can assist the Information Systems team in understanding the major functions performed by the business.

This understanding is then the foundation for the development of an information system. The information systems team understands not only the functions that occur but also the terminology used by the business in discussing the functions.

System models also serve as a communication point. In the design of a new system and the education of an existing system, the process model can help the Information Systems teams explain a system in less technical terms to the business community. If a decomposition approach is used, these models can also explain the system at various levels of detail. The major functions could be discussed in a management overview session. More detail could be provided as a system overview for general system users. The most detailed level of the model could be used by the actual users of a specific set of functions within the system.

The same system process models can also assist the Information Systems team itself. By graphically displaying the functions of the system at various levels of detail, the applications developer can get an overall picture of the application and its various components. This can assist in the application structuring and can assist in the identification of missing components early in the design process.

Information Systems teams can also use the system process models to communicate with other Information Systems teams. They can serve as the starting point for integration design. If separate development and maintenance groups are established, these models can assist in the transition from the development group to the maintenance group. New employees can also use the models to better understand the system.

It is often convenient to combine the business and system process models into a single system overview model. Not all of the activities in the business process model will be automated. Some manual activities will remain and can be documented within the information system process model to illustrate the manual activities that occur in conjunction with the automated system. In this situation, the model serves not only as a design aid to the application developer but also assists the business in redesigning procedures and perhaps entire job functions to work optimally with the proposed application.

Analyze Existing Systems

System process models can provide valuable documentation about the components of existing systems. They can highlight at a specific program level, at the programs included in an application. At a higher level, they can document the applications supported by the Information Systems group.

These models can be used by both Information Systems and the business. Management can use higher-level process models to analyze its existing portfolio of applications and target areas of improvement. Information Systems teams can use more detailed models to understand systems that they are responsible for maintaining and enhancing. The reengineering of systems can also be based on the model of the existing application.

If reverse engineering facilities are available, the development of system process models for existing systems can be a relatively simple task. A detailed system process model may be generated from existing program and job code. For example, a structure chart could be created showing the calling structure of paragraphs within a program. If standard naming conventions are in place for applications, it may also be possible to generate a higher-level model from existing information. Suppose the organization prefixes all program names with a two-character application identifier and uses the third position to identify the program as an online screen program, a report generation program, or a basic processing program. A facility could then create an information system model for the application illustrating the screens, reports, and batch programs used by the application. Since the generation of a business process model requires an understanding of the business and its terminology, it is unlikely that a true business process model could be created through reverse engineering activities.

Analyze Business Activities

The business process model primarily serves to educate the Information Systems group about the business. However, many organizations are finding business process models to be an excellent mechanism for facilating communication between business groups. Through joint model development, two diverse groups can educate each other on the specific activities they perform to help complete a business function. Often these groups can then develop an improved, more streamlined approach to handling the function.

Support Business and Information System Reorganization

From a business planning perspective, the business process model can identify the actual functions performed in the organization or a group within the organization and can thereby provide a starting point for reorganization. This may be a corporate-wide reorganization, a redistribution of job responsibilities, or the creation of new jobs to meet specific needs. For example, a process model that identifies a disproportionate number of critical activities performed by a single individual may indicate the need for an additional employee or the need for a shift of some set of responsibilities to other individuals.

Information Systems planning groups can use this same model to ensure that the Information Systems resources are correctly aligned to the business functions. The current IS structure may have been based on the business environment ten years ago. The model can highlight major application groupings that can serve as the foundation for restructured application teams. The model development process may also help Information Systems to uncover major areas of expansion or shifts in future focus that should drive their project prioritization and resource allocation process.

PROCESS MODELS IN THE LIFE CYCLE

Planning

In corporate-wide planning projects, very-high-level process models are beneficial in understanding the business as a whole. They can also be used to highlight critical areas of future development. If these models are used by the Information Systems group for strategic planning, a mapping between current systems and the future business processes can be developed to analyze how current applications meet business needs and identify new priority systems to meet critical needs.

For organizations using planning CASE tools such as KnowledgeWare's Planning Workstation, a number of other planning
objects are available such as goals, critical success factors, and
information needs. Together with processes, these objects provide a more complete picture of business directions.

Although it is helpful to use planning process models on an
enterprise-wide level, project teams can also benefit by developing a high-level process model at the start of their project. The
model can provide the Information Systems team with an understanding of the major business functions they will support. From
a business perspective, the model can help clearly document the
areas that will be addressed by the project. This helps establish
realistic expectations and ensures that the correct business resources are involved in the project from the beginning.

Analysis

In analysis, the logical process model is refined. More detail is
added as more is understood about the business. During this
phase, the model may change in its intent. The model may begin
as an illustration of the current process. However, as preparation
for a new application begins, the model should begin to reflect the
future structure of the business activities. Areas of automation
may be identified and the manual business processes may be
changed to work more efficiently with the proposed automated
functions.

Although there is somewhat of a technical emphasis at this
point, the resulting model may still be independent of the technical implementation environment. The focus is more on workflow
redesign and improvement. The end result may be a redesigned
manual process that does not necessarily require an automated
solution.

If an automated solution is selected, the business and Information Systems groups should be able to use the resulting process model to assist in their decision of an appropriate technical
platform. A complex process model may help the team divide the
project into multiple phases. The team may also elect to use a
variety of technical platforms for implementing various portions
of the model. For example, an expert system may be developed

for one segment, while a traditional CICS application may be developed for a second segment. Reporting requirements may be met by query tools in use by the business, rather than traditional systems development approaches.

Design

Information system process models are typically used to assist in the design process for traditional information systems, although many of these same concepts can be applied to other application development approaches. Initially, the business process model will be transformed into an information system process model, detailing the new automated activities to be developed. By depicting this information graphically, both the applications developer and the business representative can get an overall picture of the final application to be developed. Often by reviewing this overall model, duplications and omissions can be easily spotted.

As programs are identified, structure charts can be developed to begin designing program logic at a high level. As with the process model, the structure chart provides the developer with the opportunity graphically to review proposed structures. Generally, these are not reviewed with the business representatives, since they deal with the technical aspect of program construction.

Construction/Implementation

At this point, the process models and structure charts are refined as the system is fine-tuned for efficiency. Occasionally, major changes may be uncovered at this point that may require modifications to the business process model. Unless these changes affect manual processes only, dramatic changes may result in the information system process model and the supporting structure charts.

Maintenance

In maintenance, the structure charts can prove invaluable in helping a maintenance team member understand a program graphically before making modifications. The business and information system process models can provide new team members with an overview of the business and the application they are supporting. Enhancements that add new functionality at the program level can be easily designed through the structure chart. Larger enhancement efforts may modify the information system or business process models and the supporting structure charts.

Package Software Implementation

Process models can support both the software selection and implementation activities. A logical business process model can serve as the starting point for IS and the prospective vendors to understand the business activities to be supported by the package. Once a package has been selected, the business can use the same model to analyze potential changes to existing activities that might be required to use the new package.

System process models could also be developed at the logical and physical levels for the package. Physical models depicting program structure would be helpful for individuals enhancing the delivered software. These models could be easily developed from delivered documentation and source code, if available. Logical system process models can help visualize the overall structure of the system itself, possibly including online navigation paths and the contents of job streams. These logical process models may be easier to develop than the logical data models since vendors generally provide high-level diagrams of their software processing that can be manually translated into system process models.

REQUIREMENTS FOR PROCESS MODEL MAINTENANCE

Maintaining Business Process Models

Although process models tend to be simpler in structure than data models and include a very limited number of object types, their maintenance can be difficult. The primary hindrance is the lack of standardization in process names. Most developers prefer to create process models in a JAD session environment where the processes are named by the business community. It is difficult to enforce defined naming standards in this environment. Not only does it restrict the creativity of the model definition, but it also limits the business-oriented philosophy of business process model development.

If the organization is using a CASE tool that merges based on object names, this issue of process model naming must be addressed. One option is to establish naming standards that ensure uniqueness at least at the system process model level. A numbering convention is often used for business processes to provide uniqueness in the process name while easily identifying the position of the process within the model. If the organization feels that naming standards are too restrictive, duplicate names can be identified at the time of model merging and can be differentiated at that time.

Ensuring name uniqueness may be the easiest part of business process model maintenance. Ensuring continued model accuracy is more difficult. If the business makes a change, they often do not inform the Information Systems group that the change has been made. If they do, the Information Systems group may not have the time or the business understanding required to update the business process model correctly. For this reason, it is best to let the business have ownership of its business process models and to be held responsible for model maintenance. In many environments, this additional expectation of the business is unrealistic unless the business itself utilizes the models and therefore requires them to be correct. An alternative is to maintain these models only at the start of a new project or major enhancement that requires the use of accurate models.

Since KnowledgeWare merges models based on object names, the naming of processes is critical to successful model management. Prefixes, including numbering to identify levels in the model, can be useful but are difficult to maintain as the model is changed. As with logical data models, the model manager must be familiar with the names of the processes and the business meaning to ensure model integrity. Using definitions and comments can therefore be very helpful in assisting the model manager in identifying duplicate processes. Due to the relative simplicity of the Decomposition Diagrammer tool, it is possible to train the business on the tool and let the business be directly responsible for maintaining the model. The model manager then becomes a support person who provides assistance with the technical aspects of model merging.

Maintaining System Process Models

System process model developers face the same challenge. When modeling a detailed set of programs and modules, the organization usually has standards the developer can follow. However, the use of seven- or eight-character cryptic names limits the audience of the model. If the developer instead uses business terms as a part of the name, he gains business understanding but may sacrifice uniqueness in his process model names. A compromise may be as simple as prefixing each process or module with the standard module identifier, followed by the business term for the function.

At this physical level, it is important to ensure that the modules are not only unique, but that they accurately reflect the system that is in place. Including the actual program or routine name as a part of the process or module name provides an easy mechanism for manual or automated verification. However, name checking cannot ensure that the system structure has not been altered without changing the supporting process model. Procedures must be established wherein any changes to the system are implemented within the system process model, preferably prior to implementing the system changes.

In an organization moving toward reusable subroutines accessible within projects, across projects, or even across applications, ensuring that the system model is accurate becomes even more important. Multiple projects may be using the same routine. Some may even be making modifications that will affect other projects. Close control over the use and modification of these routines becomes a critical model management activity. This involves tracking which projects are using the routine, which are making changes, and which completed projects may be affected by the change.

There is no automatic facility provided within the Knowledge-Ware tool to ensure the validity of the physical process model. Some other vendors are providing reverse engineering tools that

will generate the appropriate objects within the design workstation to document an existing program or entire system. This leaves
a void for the model manager to fill. An option is to create a report
of existing modules and processes and compare this to a list of
programs currently in use. If naming standards are identical in
KnowledgeWare and in the final code, this verification could be
easily automated.

Maintaining Process Model Linkages

By maintaining the linkage between the business process model
and the system process model, the organization can easily identify the portions of the system that support a part of the business.
If this part of the business changes, the Information Systems
group can isolate for more detailed analysis the portions of the
system that will potentially be affected. When a system change is
planned, the Information Systems group can better identify the
business groups that need to be involved in the analysis and
design of the change.

KnowledgeWare provides a linkage between a process and a
module. If processes are used to document the business model
and modules are used to document the information system model,
this relationship provides the required linkage. However, some
organizations decide to document both the business model and the
high-level information system model using processes. In this case,
linkages can be made by using the same name for both objects but
prefixing or suffixing the system process name, or by using the
definition or comments to detail the relationship.

A new feature available in Release 2.7 is a Process Transla-
tor. This facility creates a structure chart from a process decomposition diagram and from portions of the dataflow diagram, if
available. This feature automatically creates the linkage between the logical process and the physical module. If the logical
design is changed, the physical design can either be regenerated
or manually changed. The regeneration option is best in situations where no changes have been made to the physical design
after the generation or where the changes are so dramatic that
any changes made only to the physical are no longer valid and
must be replaced. Since the translation works similarly to a con-

solidation, this is an activity in which the model manager should play an active role.

INFORMATION MODELS FOR PROCESS MODELING OBJECTS

The types of objects included in the process portion of the information model will depend on the levels of process models the firm is developing and maintaining and the approach the CASE tool vendor takes to supporting process models. A standard process model is shown in Figure 4.4. In this model, a function represents an object in the conceptual business process model. A function may be decomposed into another function. A process represents an object in the business process model. It may also be decomposed into another process. Applications, programs, and modules represent other detailed objects in the system process model. Linkages that are maintained include the function and process and the process and module.

Developing a Customized Process Information Model

Since each organization will approach process modeling in a slightly different manner, based on the methodology, CASE tools, and data model goals in place, each organization will have its own unique process information model. The following questions are designed to assist the organization in developing an initial process information model. After this initial model is complete, the organization will need to identify which objects and relationships are required, which are optional, and which properties apply to each object.

1. Will the conceptual process model be maintained?

If so, add an entity for each object used to store conceptual processes. Examples are Functions, Information Needs, Goals, Critical Success Factors, and Processes.

2. What are the relationships between these conceptual data objects?

Add relationship lines indicating relationships between conceptual objects. For example, if a Function contains many Processes,

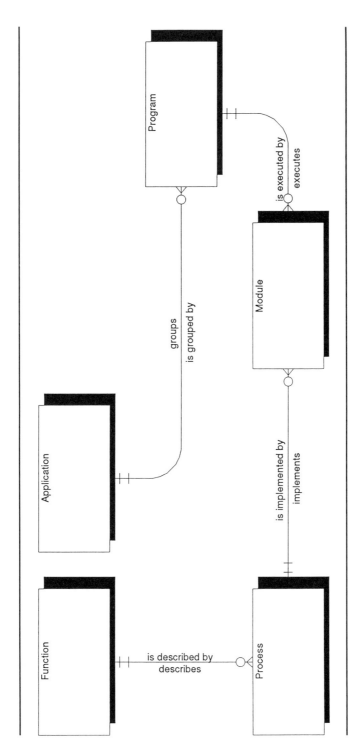

Figure 4.4. Entity Relationship Diagrammer : process information model.

draw a one-to-many relationship line between Function and Process. If a Process can be a part of many Functions, change the relationship to a many-to-many relationship.

3. Will the logical process model be maintained?

If so, add an entity for each object used to store logical processes. Examples are Processes, Logical Screens, Logical Reports, and Logical Programs.

4. What are the relationships between logical process objects?

Add relationship lines indicating relationships between logical objects. For example, if a process contains many logical programs, draw a one-to-many relationship between process and logical programs. If a logical program can implement multiple processes, change the relationship to a many-to-many.

In some methodologies, processes can be decomposed into processes. This means a process can contain other processes. Often one process can be a part of a decomposition for more than one process. The resulting relationship would be a many-to-many relationship from the process entity to the process entity.

5. Will the physical data model be maintained?

If so, add an entity for each object used to store physical processes. Examples are Programs, Modules, and Subroutines. In identifying these objects, it is helpful to consider objects that are tracked by tools other than traditional CASE tools such as source management packages.

6. What are the relationships between physical data objects?

In a simplistic environment that is not implementing reusable modules of code, the only physical objects tracked will be programs and no relationships will be required. However, if programs are broken down into modules, add a one-to-many relationship from program to module. If a module can be used in multiple programs, change the relationship to a many-to-many relationship.

In some cases programs are not broken down into modules, but programs can call other programs. To illustrate this calling structure, add a one-to-many relationship from program to program. If a strict hierarchy is not in place and the same program can both call many programs and be called by more than one program, change the relationship to a many-to-many relationship.

7. Is there a need to identify which logical processes comprise a conceptual process?

If so, a one-to-many relationship should be added between the appropriate conceptual process object and the process. If any process can be contained in multiple occurrences of the conceptual process object, the relationship should be a many-to-many relationship.

8. Is there a need to compare the logical model to its physical implementation?

If so, a relationship is needed to help track the physical version of the logical model. In many cases, this relationship could be a one-to-many relationship between the process and a physical process object, such as a program or module, indicating that one process could be implemented by multiple programs or modules. If the physical process object can implement multiple processes, the relationship should be changed to many-to-many.

9. Will details be maintained about logical processes as well as physical programs?

It is important to determine the purpose of logical processes and physical programs. If details such as purposes and descriptions are maintained about both, it is possible that some redundancy may exist. It is important to distinguish clearly between the details kept at each level. For example, logical processes may reflect the business definition, while programs reflect the technical definition. Other areas of the model that are linked, such as the conceptual process objects and the logical process objects, should also be evaluated for similar redundancies of detailed properties.

The approach outlined through these questions creates a basic information model, such as that shown in Figure 4.4. It is only one possible approach to information model development. An experienced data analyst in the organization can customize these questions and the resulting instructions to match the data analysis techniques in use by the organization. In this approach, no attempt was made to develop a fully normalized data model since the purpose was to identify basic business requirements. If the organization wishes to use the resulting model to build a repository structure, additional refinement may be required.

ACTIVITY MODELS FOR PROCESS MODEL MANAGEMENT

The activity model for process model management illustrates the major tasks to be performed in managing process objects and their linkages. A sample activity model is displayed in Figure 4.5. This model divides activities into major groups based on the types of functions the model manager performs. Identifying objects, linkages, and associated standards is viewed as one major function. Providing all necessary groups with access to the models is a second. The third functional grouping includes major tasks required to ensure the validity of the models.

Figure 4.6 illustrates how the information model is used to ensure that the process models reflect the business and existing systems. The business process model objects, here identified as functions and processes, can be validated by two mechanisms, business plans and a business review team. The production source library is the validation point for programs and modules. By documenting this type of detail in the activity model, the requirements and procedures of model management can be detailed.

Developing a Customized Process Activity Model

Just as each organization will have its own information model, it will also have its own activity model. The structure of the activity model will likely differ based on the way in which the organization assigns responsibility for model management activities. The specific tasks will also differ since each organization will have different

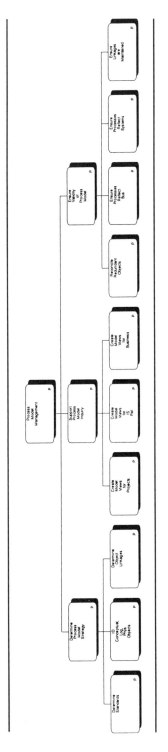

Figure 4.5. Decomposition Diagrammer : process model management.

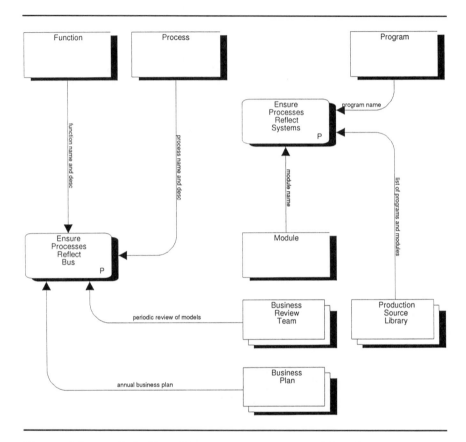

Figure 4.6.   Data Flow Diagrammer : ensure validity of process
model.

priorities as well as different objects to be managed. The following
questions have been designed to assist the organization in developing an initial process activity model. The emphasis at this stage
should be on identifying the required tasks. In later chapters, options for organizing the model will be discussed.

1. Who will use the models?

The audience of the models determines what types of access need
to be provided by the model management team. If the models are
only used by the Information Systems group in conjunction with
project activities, the model management tasks may be based

around the organization's project development life cycle. However, if the models are needed for basic inquiry by the business or the Information Systems staff, more tasks may be required to make these models easily available.

2. When will they need access to the models?

If immediate access is required at any time, the model manager needs to provide facilities for user access of models. If the access is known in advance, the model manager can personally process requests for models and provide manual control of the models. By identifying the different situations in which access will be required, the model manager can better define detailed procedures that meet the needs of the model users.

3. How will conceptual and logical models be verified?

The activities required to ensure valid models are critical to model management. It is important that mechanisms are established to ensure that the models are valid. Possible mechanisms are shown in Figure 4.6.

4. How will physical models be verified?

Most organizations utilize source management software that tracks details of programs. This software can provide important input into the verification of physical models. An automated facility is optimal, but a manual procedure of comparing the contents of the repository to the source management software is feasible.

These are some of the major issues to be evaluated in developing the activity model. Each organization will identify activities specific to process model management as it gains experience in model development, usage, and management.

5. How will Process Translation be managed (for users of Release 2.7 and above)?

If the new Process Translation feature is used, model management will need to define carefully the parameters of how subsequent translations are made. Situations where the entire model should be retranslated, where only portions of the model should be retranslated, and where manual maintenance should be performed instead of the translation should be outlined. During the first few projects, it may be helpful for the model management team to specify that they are to be responsible for the translation, to gain experience in the types of issues involved and to fully define the organization's direction.

5

Techniques for Linking Process and Data Models

DEFINITION OF LINKAGE MODELS

Linkage models illustrate the relationship between the data model and the process model. They may take very different forms, from a simple cross-reference table to a detailed specification. The type of linkage model used depends on the phase of development and the level of analysis or design required.

The primary purpose of linkage models is to help verify both the data model and the process model. If processes have been defined but reference no data, an omission may have occurred during data model development. Conversely, a data object that is not used by any processes indicates extra data or a missing process.

In addition to providing this cross reference, linkage models can assist the further analysis or development of the system. A model such as a dataflow diagram or a specification that explains how data is used by a process may help the developer in better understanding the system and its flow. From a business model perspective, linkage models can add additional detail about the flow of data among business processes.

MATRICES

A matrix is the easiest approach to documenting a relationship between a data and a process model. The matrix at a conceptual level would show which data groups were used by which high-level business functions. The data group EMPLOYEE may be used by the business functions Process Payroll, Hire Employees, and Provide Benefits. Such a model is useful in identifying data that crosses business functions and therefore requires special control. For example, the matrix would highlight that changes to EMPLOYEE information may affect the Payroll, Recruitment, and Benefits functions.

At a logical modeling level, the matrix can depict which entities are used by which business processes. The matrix can assist in validating both the data model and the process model by identifying data that is not used in any processes and processes that do not have the required data (Figure 5.1). If an EMPLOYEE ADDRESS entity had been defined as required information, but no process existed to create it, either a new function must be added or an existing function must be expanded. Another alternative is for the business to decide that EMPLOYEE ADDRESS is not a critical piece of business information at this time. Such additions, changes, and deletions to both models can be identified early in the life cycle.

Although it is possible to build a matrix between attributes and processes, such a detailed model would be time-consuming to develop and maintain. However, for detailed analysis of a select group of attributes and their use in the system, it may be a worthwhile exercise. In defining an inventory system, it may be helpful

	Setup a New Employee	Terminate an Employee	Train an Employee	Transfer an Employee
Employee	✓	✓	✓	✓
Employee Address				
Employee Job	✓			✓
Employee Training			✓	

Figure 5.1.   Association Matrix Diagrammer : employee management.

to look at the specific inventory quantities that are planned for the system and to track their creation, update, and retrieval by processes both within the scope of the system and outside of the system itself. ONHAND INVENTORY QUANTITY may be used and updated by multiple applications, including Order Processing and Manufacturing. INTRANSIT INVENTORY QUANTITY may only be maintained by the Distribution system and therefore may be more easily controlled.

Matrices at the physical level are much less common since the information contained in the matrix can be determined from other locations, such as program code. However, a matrix at the data structure/program module level can be helpful in analyzing frequently used data structures and identifying data-intensive modules. Documentation of the number of online modules that will access the PRODUCT file may affect the Database Administrator's decision of how to organize the file. For program development and maintenance planning, it may be helpful to know that a specific program accesses five high-use database files. The matrix can also assist in scheduling jobs to minimize data contention.

CASE tools that support matrices can greatly assist the analyst in understanding data and process relationships. Like most other models, matrices were rarely used in the past due to the difficult in initially creating and maintaining them. In tools that can automatically generate a list of processes and entities and possibly predefine some relationships based on other diagrams, the matrix can prove to be a good analysis and review document.

KnowledgeWare's Planning Workstation allows for extensive use of matrices in project planning and analysis. A predefined set of objects that can be associated is provided. Some of these associations allow the documentation of additional information about the relationship. For example, an estimated volume of the number of occurrences of an entity used by each process can be documented. The matrix is automatically built from existing objects and new objects can be added, based on rules within the tool. Therefore, management of these matrices is relatively straightforward.

As mentioned in Chapter 3, KnowledgeWare Release 2.7 offers expanded functionality in the use of matrices. The straightforward association matrix described above is still available, but is now enhanced by a Reporting Association Matrix, which allows the use of traceable associations. From a linkage standpoint, new associations could be viewed without being directly maintained. For example, Processes could be linked to the Information Needs that were defined for the process. Information Needs could be linked to the entities that supported them. Processes could then be linked indirectly to Entities, based on Information Needs. This new flexibility offers organizations a great deal of options in how they identify and document linkage associations.

ENTITY LIFE CYCLE ANALYSIS

A special type of matrix that may be developed for logical data and process models is the Entity Life Cycle matrix. As the name implies, this matrix relates entities to processes based on the action the process performs on the entity. Four standard actions are generally used: Create, Retrieve, Update, and Delete. A process may perform any or all of these actions on the entity (Figure 5.2).

The purpose of entity life cycle analysis is to ensure that a process exists to perform all necessary functions on the entity.

	Setup a New Employee	Terminate an Employee	Train an Employee	Transfer an Employee
Employee	C	U	R	R
Employee Address				
Employee Job	C			DC
Employee Training			CU	

Figure 5.2.   Association Matrix Diagrammer : employee management.

C : 1 or more instances are created.
R : 1 or more instances are retrieved.
U : 1 or more instances are updated.
D : 1 or more instances are deleted.

For example, an entity may be read by several processes but no process may exist to create the entity. This tells the analyst that a creation process is missing or the entity represents existing information maintained by another system. The matrix can assist not only system developers but can also assist the business community in analyzing their current information flow.

KnowledgeWare automatically builds the foundation for the entity life cycle matrix in its Entity to Process association matrix. Actions can then be added by the analyst. Since the tool builds this matrix from the list of defined entities and processes, it automatically maintains the matrix with name changes, additions, and deletions.

DATAFLOW DIAGRAMMING

Dataflow diagrams are graphical illustrations of data that is input to and output from processes. At the conceptual level, a dataflow diagram can identify the major uses of data groups as input or output to major business functions. The diagram helps the business visualize the flow of information through the enterprise. A logical dataflow diagram depicts the business flow at a lower level of detail. Physical dataflow diagrams illustrate the way specific modules use data structures.

Traditional dataflow diagrams contain four basic types of objects. A process may be a business function, a logical business activity, or a specific module. A data store represents a collection of data, which may or may not equate to a data object in the data model. An external agent represents an object outside of the boundary of the system or process being analyzed that sends information to or receives information from a data store or process. Examples of external agents are the Payroll department, a Customer Service agent, or an interface system. A dataflow is either an inflow or outflow of information between the objects of the dataflow diagram. Rules for which objects the dataflow may connect differ widely by the modeling technique used.

A sample dataflow diagram is shown in Figure 5.3. The conventions used in this model are rounded boxes for processes, three-sided boxes for data stores, double boxes for external agents, and arrowed lines for dataflows. The direction of the arrow indicates

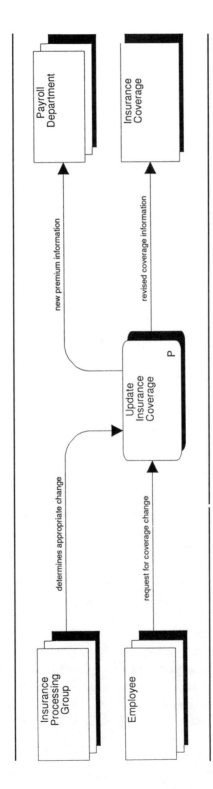

Figure 5.3. Data Flow Diagrammer : insurance update.

the direction of dataflow. The example shown is a Human Resources insurance update system. The employee sends a form to the insurance group; both the employee and the insurance group are represented by external agents. The insurance group then updates the insurance coverage data store and sends the new premium information to the Payroll department.

Processes, External Agents, Data Flows, Data Stores, and Junctions are the objects provided by KnowledgeWare for dataflow diagramming. The tool includes some basic edits, such as not allowing a dataflow between two data stores. Warnings are provided for some situations that may be errors in some methodologies, such as external agents added at detailed dataflow diagrams. Analysts must know whether they can ignore these types of errors. If additional dataflow diagramming restrictions are used by the organization, models must be manually reviewed.

Linkage to the Process Model

A process in a dataflow diagram is a process from the process model. Whether each process participates in a dataflow diagram depends on the modeling methodology used. A dataflow diagram can be developed at each level of the diagram or only for selected levels, such as the lowest levels. Analysts may elect to develop dataflow diagrams for only those portions of the process model that they feel need additional evaluation.

Some dataflow diagrammers use the dataflowing activity as a way of developing their process model. The modeling activity begins with the identification of a single process, the system or business area being analyzed, with inputs and outputs of data. The process is then broken down into finer levels of detail in a lower-level dataflow diagram with multiple processes. Subsequent dataflow diagrams are then developed for the intermediate level of processes. In this method, the decomposition diagram discussed in Chapter 4 can be developed.

Dataflow diagrams can also be developed at the module level. In this case, the processes represented in the diagram are actually modules in the physical design. The CASE tool may either allow the module object itself to be used in the diagram or may require the developer to create a logical process model that includes linkages between processes and modules.

KnowledgeWare's dataflow diagrammer and process decomposition diagrammer are tightly related. Dataflow diagrams are maintained for a specific process. If a process is added on the dataflow diagram, the same process is added as a child of the dataflow diagram topic process. If a process is added as a child of the process, it automatically appears on the dataflow diagram for the process. Deletes and name changes are handled by the same method. Therefore, model managers do not need to ensure conformance between the process model and the dataflow diagram from a process perspective.

Linkage to the Data Model

While the relationship between the dataflow diagram and the process model is relatively straightforward, a variety of options exist for linking the data model to the dataflow diagram. The simplest approach is to allow each data store to represent an entity on the logical data model. Visually, the relationship is easily identifiable to all reviewers. However, this simple approach does not provide the level of detail that many dataflow diagrammers seek.

Another alternative is to allow a data store to represent only that information that is stored. Using this approach, the data store may represent a single attribute from one entity, a group of attributes from one entity, or a collection of attributes from multiple entities. Some CASE tools allow such subsets of the data model to be linked to data stores on the dataflow diagram. Although the information may not be readily available by reviewing the dataflow diagram itself, supporting documentation in the form of "where-used" reports or subsets of data models can provide the necessary detail.

A dataflow, or the relationship between a process and a data store or external agent, may also be used to relate the data model to the dataflow diagram. The flow may represent a conceptual data group, one or more entities, or specific attributes from one or more entities. The relationship may be made through dataflow naming, by placing the names of the data objects on the dataflow, or by creating a subset of the data model and assigning it to the dataflow through the use of the tool.

Some tools also facilitate the assigning of a portion of the data model to a process object. This approach directly links the data and the process model together and makes reporting of the relationship easy. However, if this approach alone is used for relating data and process objects, the use of the dataflows and data stores within the diagram must be carefully investigated. They may not in fact add additional value to the model, and the analyst should instead consider the use of matrices.

If the dataflow diagram is at a physical level, the data object linkages may be to specific data structures or data elements. The same concepts of linking to data objects still apply.

KnowledgeWare supports many of these approaches to linking the entity model to a dataflow diagram. Views of the data model can be created for dataflows, data stores, and processes. Entity deletions and name changes will automatically be reflected in the view, but additions must be handled manually since the tool does not know which views will use the new entity. Some organizations elect not to take the additional step of creating the view of the entity model and instead use a naming convention that makes linkage possible.

Maintaining Dataflow Diagrams

Although CASE tools have greatly facilitated the development of dataflow diagrams, tools differ in how well they support accurate maintenance. Most tools do use the same process objects in the process models and dataflow diagrams. However, the approach the tool and the user take to linking data models to the diagram may affect the automatic maintainability of the model. If the data store and the entity are the same object, according to both the tool and the user, a change to an entity will automatically be reflected in the dataflow diagram. Other mechanisms of linking the two models make automatic maintenance by the tool difficult, and manual changes are usually required.

Unless the dataflow diagram is linked in some way to resulting specifications, it is also difficult to maintain the flows and their directions automatically. No tool can automatically change external agents when an organizational change occurs. Therefore, most CASE tool users will be required to maintain manually their dataflow diagrams in some form if they are to be used long-term.

KnowledgeWare's required linkage of the process model and dataflow diagrams eases the burden on model managers. If views of the entity model are used, the model manager can request a report that will list all the places an entity is used as a part of a view. This highlights areas where maintenance may be required and can narrow the scope of model verification. If the organization did not use views but used some form of consistent naming, such as identical entity and data store names, it would be feasible to easily develop a facility that validates the linkage between the data model and dataflow diagram. As this case illustrates, the advantages of allowing the tool to perform some automatic maintenance and integrity checking should be weighed against the cost of maintaining the linkage and the time required to develop procedures to verify linkages outside the boundaries of the tool itself.

SPECIFICATIONS

Specifications for a process, program, or a module called by a program can also be used to link data models and process models. Lower CASE tools use some form of specification, which may be freeform text in a noncode generation environment or pseudocode for code generation, to document the detailed processing of a module. Although the format of these specifications varies widely among CASE tools, the linkage aspects are virtually identical.

A sample specification is shown in Figure 5.4. This diagram illustrates a sample text-based specification for the process included in the dataflow diagram in Figure 5.3. Examples of data accesses and called modules are included in this specification.

The mini-spec diagrammer in KnowledgeWare's Analysis Workstation allows the documentation of details for processes, while the module action diagrammer in the Design Workstation allows the documentation of details for modules. Both tools allow the developer to enter text, which may be in a pseudocode format. If Knowledge-

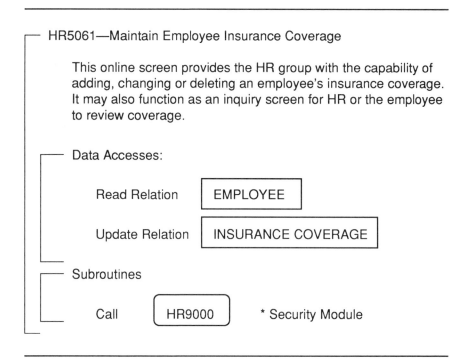

HR5061—Maintain Employee Insurance Coverage

This online screen provides the HR group with the capability of adding, changing or deleting an employee's insurance coverage. It may also function as an inquiry screen for HR or the employee to review coverage.

Data Accesses:

Read Relation   EMPLOYEE

Update Relation   INSURANCE COVERAGE

Subroutines

Call   HR9000   * Security Module

Figure 5.4.   Module Action Diagrammer : Module HR5061

Ware's code generation facility is used, the pseudocode must conform to the standard used by the Construction Workstation. The tool automatically links the process and module to its specification, but the model manager must manually ensure that the specification matches the final program. This can be accomplished for detailed specifications through the use of controlled procedures that do not allow maintenance of the generated program code and only allow changes directly to the specification stored in the CASE tool.

Process Model Linkage

The specification is developed for a specific program, module, or process. Therefore, the specification is automatically linked to the appropriate process object. If a structure chart was used to graphically depict the module calling structure, a change in the calling structure at the specification level may cause a change to the supporting structure chart if the tool integrates specification diagrams with structure chart diagrams.

In the sample specification (Figure 5.4), the name of the specification is used to link the specification to the program it supports. The security module is a called subroutine. The tool in this example tracks the linkage to the subroutine through the reference in the specification.

Data Model Linkage

Most tools support the linkage of the physical data model to the specification in some form. It may be a specific reference to a database access that provides a link at the data structure level. Other tools may support the reference of specific data elements, providing a more detailed link.

If the tool does not explicitly allow a linkage to the data model, the tool user can create a manual linkage by using the data structure or data element name directly within the specification. This provides the benefit of where-used information, although it may be more difficult to search through all specifications to obtain it. If the tool does not provide a true linkage, it is also difficult to maintain changes in physical data object names.

Figure 5.4 illustrates tool-supported linkage to data objects, in this case physical data structures. This linkage is not at the data element level, but does explain the type of access to the data structure itself.

Prior to Release 2.7, KnowledgeWare allowed a module action diagram to reference a specific data structure through a defined data access. This linkage allowed the tool to automatically update the specification when a name change occurred to the physical data structure. It also provided the model manager with visibility of the use of specific data structures, assisting in the change analysis process.

Release 2.7 allows linkage at a lower data element level, providing even more automation in model management. The data element level may be a local or global data structure or a catalog attribute used within a physical data structure, such as a screen variable.

Maintaining Specifications

In code generation environments, ensuring the validity of the specification is vital since the actual program is developed directly from the specification. If the organization maintains only specifications and never modifies generated source code, specification maintenance is ensured as a natural byproduct of program maintenance since it is the program maintenance. Data and process linkages will also be kept up to date as a result of the maintenance process.

However, organizations that are not yet generating code or are allowing maintenance to generated source code will find themselves in the same specification maintenance dilemma organizations have had for years. The only difference is that CASE tools may have made it easier to develop more detailed specifications, which in turn may be even harder to maintain.

In considering specification maintenance, it is important for the noncode generation organization to evaluate the importance of specification maintenance. If the main goal is to provide where-used information, this same information may be easily retrievable from the actual program source. If the organization hopes to transition to code generation in the future and expects to be able to use existing specifications as a foundation, the accuracy of the specification may be more critical. However, as reverse engineering of program code becomes an increasingly viable technology, it may prove easier to generate a specification from existing code as needed than to maintain a detailed specification. From a model maintenance perspective it may be simplest to maintain high-level specifications that provide an overview of the processing logic and the data model accesses, perhaps at the data structure level.

SCREEN AND REPORT LAYOUTS

Screen and Report layout facilities in many CASE tools offer the ability to assign data elements to a screen or report and then detail the associated processing. These diagrammers make user involvement in the detailed system design feasible and often incorporate system prototyping capabilities that allow a simulation of the system with sample data and navigation.

A sample screen layout is shown in Figure 5.5. This screen could be displayed as a function of the specification described in Figure 5.4. It shows the business-defined layout of the screen that supports employee insurance coverage maintenance.

The KnowledgeWare Design Workstation provides a Screen Layout tool that allows the developer to create the screen or report layout. The screen can then be referenced by a module, providing process model linkage, and can use the same data structures defined for the physical data model. Even if the screen layout itself is not maintained to be identical to the screen actually implemented with the system, the basic cross-reference information, if maintained, can prove vital in providing total system documentation.

Linkage to Process Models

Screens and Reports may either represent a process themselves, with detailed logic linked directly to them, or they may be refer-

```
XXXXXXXX              Employee Insurance Coverage        page 99 of 99


SSN              999999999            Employee Type   X   XXXXXXXXXXXXXXXXXXX
Employee Name    XXXXXXXXXXXXXXXXXXX  Employee Status  XX  XXXXXXXXXXXXXXXXXXX
Work Location    XXXX XXXXXXXXXXXXXXXXXXX

      Ins Type    Coverage Type   Eligible       Coverage Dates       Premium

   X    XXXXX        XXXXX         XXXXXXXX     XXXXXXXX to XXXXXXXX    S99999999




Message  XXXXXXXXXXXXXXXXXXXXXXXXXXXXXXXXXXXXXXXXXXXXXXXXXXXXXXXXXXXXXXXXXXXXXXXX
```

Figure 5.5.   Screen Layout Diagrammer : update insurance coverage.

enced within a specification, which is linked to a process, pro-gram, or module. KnowledgeWare links the screen or report to a module through the Action Diagrammer, or specification. A Get or Put command is added within the Action Diagram to docu-ment the linkage. The end result is easy automated linkage of the screen or report object to the appropriate process-oriented object.

Linkage to Data Models

CASE tools that support both data modeling and process model-ing often allow the direct linkage of the physical data model to the screen or report layout. This may be by directly using the data elements defined in the data structure as components of the screen. If the tool does not provide this level of integration, it may allow the definition of screen-specific data elements, which can be linked to the data structure data elements, either as a part of the layout activity or as a part of the specification development.

The sample screen layout shown in Figure 5.5 illustrates how data elements may be directly referenced by the screen layout. The field lengths and formats were based on the data element's definition in the physical data model. This would provide for au-tomatic screen maintenance if a change were made to the charac-teristics of the data model.

If the vendor does not provide a linkage between data elements and the layout, one can be created either through specifications or by using comments that specify the corresponding physical data element name for each field on the layout. As with other non-automated forms of linkage, either of these two approaches will increase the maintenance problems resulting from changes to the layout or the database. Compiling and analyzing the where-used type of information will also be more complex.

As mentioned above, the KnowledgeWare tool does allow the use of lowest-level physical data structures directly on the screen. If correctly implemented, changes to data elements such as name changes and field length changes can be automatically reflected on the Screen and Report layout. However, if procedures allow devel-opers to define special formats for screen displays, the model man-ager must have a set of rules in place ensuring that the developer does not change the actual definition of the physical data element. A procedure should also be established so that special versions of data elements developed for screen display can be linked back to the physical data element definition.

LINKAGES IN THE LIFE CYCLE

Planning

Linkages can be helpful in the planning stage to identify how data is used within the organization's major processes. This can assist in the determination of critical data areas based on future business directions. The planning team can then assess whether existing data can support these critical areas or if new or expanded databases are required.

Linkages also assist the Information Systems and business teams in understanding at a high level how data flows through the organization. For example, it might highlight the usage of product information by most major functions of the business: Product Development, Marketing, Manufacturing, and Distribution. Coordination points for data design and modification can be easily identified.

Matrices and dataflow diagrams are the most commonly used linkages in the planning phase. Matrices may be preferred when detailed information about how data flows is not available, but the access of data by a process is known. Dataflow diagrams have the advantage of graphically depicting the flow of information, but do require an understanding of whether data is used as input, output, or both input and output for a process.

Analysis

During the analysis phase, linkage models can help the business and the Information Systems team better understand the current or proposed flow of information for a specific project. This flow may represent the flow within business processes or among the proposed components of a new system. Adjustments to proposed flows can be made easily using the diagramming capabilities of CASE tools.

In addition to assisting the project team in analyzing the use of data by processes, linkage models can help to validate the data and process models. If data was defined in the data model but is not linked to any processes, either the data is unnecessary or processes are missing. Conversely, if the required data for a process is not defined in the data model, either the process is misunderstood or data is missing in the data model.

Dataflow diagrams are the most commonly used linkages in this phase. As in the planning phase, the graphical representations can assist the project team in visualizing the business and the proposed system. Matrices, especially entity life cycle matrices, can also be helpful at this stage by providing direct linkages between data and processes. Some methodologies may use high-level specifications near the end of this phase to provide linkages between data and processes.

Screen layouts are also used by some analysts during this phase as a mechanism for data review within the business. In environments where the business community is not actively using end-user computing tools such as spreadsheets and fourth-generation languages, they may have difficulty understanding information independent of a specific application. By creating a screen layout that shows the major keys of an entity and all its non-key attributes, the data design can be effectively presented. To identify relationships between data entities, the information could be displayed in an appropriate screen format. For example, if a Product has many Vendors, a screen layout could be designed that has the Product Identifier and other descriptive product information at the top and a repeating group of Vendor information, including the Vendor Identifier and Name. Although this approach is beneficial in certain circumstances, it may not be advisable for all projects since it gives the business the impression that the system is nearing completion while it is still in the analysis phase, and it tends to disassociate the business from the actual identification and design of screens.

Design

As the system itself is detailed during the design phase, the opportunity to track linkages can provide vital information to a project.

Generally during this phase, multiple designers are working concurrently. If linkages are available, the potential impact of data changes can be easily analyzed and all designers can be appropriately informed of the changes.

Linkages can also assist the Database Administration group in analyzing database performance. Data that is used in multiple online transactions may be designed differently from data used by a single batch program. The type of access, whether it be inquiry or update, can also be analyzed.

Screen and Report layouts and specifications are the most common linkage models used during the design phase. Dataflow diagrams may also be used to help illustrate the inputs and outputs of a specific program module. Major system changes may necessitate a change to models developed in earlier phases, including the matrices.

Construction

During this final project phase, the linkage models may be updated if the system design changes. The dataflow diagrams can prove helpful in planning the implementation strategy, since they illustrate the required inputs and outputs of each process and can therefore identify sequencing requirements.

Maintenance

All types of linkage models can be helpful for maintenance teams. Since they provide where-used information, a data change can easily be assessed at both a logical and physical level if these models are maintained as system changes occur. The conceptual and logical linkage models can be helpful in assisting both the business and new information systems team members in understanding the system. For major enhancements, the models can be a starting point for analyzing new features and their impact on the existing data and processes.

Package Software Implementation

Linkage models can be helpful in planning package software implementation. If provided by the vendor or easily obtainable through reverse engineering, they can help in sequencing implementation. Perhaps a more beneficial use of linkage models for software package implementation is the development of an interface strategy. Most purchased software must interface with existing data structures. By identifying the flow of information to and from the package, the analysis and design of these interfaces can be facilitated. Dataflow diagrams and matrices are the most commonly used linkage models in this scenario.

LINKAGE INFORMATION MODELS

The information model that supports the linkage of data and process objects will be specific to the types of objects linked together and the technique selected for linkage. The basic model for linkage was shown in Chapter 2, Figure 2.1. In this model, logical data and process objects were linked and physical data structures and program modules were linked. The details of how this linkage occurs is the issue in developing the linkage portion of the information model.

If a simple cross-reference matrix is used, the linkage may be represented by a new entity, Data Process Cross Reference. This entity would be needed if the organization allows a data object to be used by multiple processes and a process object to access multiple data objects. At a more detailed level, the organization needs to determine which specific objects the linkage should occur for. The entity to process linkage is the basic relationship, shown in Figure 5.6 using a matrix to track the linkage. Other possibilities include an attribute to process linkage and a data group to process linkage.

This same type of model also applies to screens, reports, and specifications. Assuming once again that a process-oriented object can access multiple data objects and data can be used by multiple process objects, three new entities could be added. The data structure screen cross reference and data structure report cross reference would track linkages through screens and reports to physical data structures. This linkage could also occur at the data element level. In the case of specifications, the linkage entity could be between the data structure and the program module, the entity and the process for logical specifications, and the data element and the program module. Any linkages tracked at the data element level

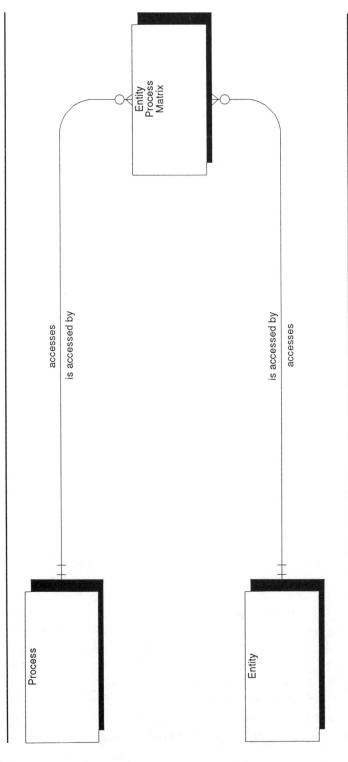

Figure 5.6. Entity Relationship Diagrammer : logical data process link via matrix.

would also require identification of the physical data structure that contains the data element if data elements are not unique across the physical data structures. A basic information model for these linkages is shown in Figure 5.7.

If dataflow diagrams are used, several new objects may be added to the information model. Using the generic object types discussed above, entities for Data Stores, External Agents and Dataflows would be defined. If Data Stores represented one and only one entity, the data store object could be omitted from the diagram. Otherwise, relationships would be added from the entity or attribute to the data store. If one data store could represent multiple entities or attributes and the entity or attribute could be represented by many data stores, an entity data store or attribute data store object would be included (Figure 5.8). If dataflows or processes were the source of linkage to the data model, a similar type of relationship could be added.

Developing a Customized Linkage Information Model

Since organizations have their own unique data and process information models, the way in which they link these models will also be unique. The following questions are designed to assist the organization in bringing together its data and process information models into a single organization information model. After these additions to the initial model are complete, the organization will need to identify which of the new objects and relationships are required, which are optional, and which properties apply to each new object.

1. Will matrices be maintained?

Matrices are helpful to both the development and maintenance processes. However, if the CASE tools in use do not provide for automatic update of matrices when a change occurs, the realistic benefit of matrix maintenance must be considered. If the Employee entity name is changed to Active Employee and the change is not automatically reflected on the matrix, someone will need to make the correction manually. If the team uses the matrix to analyze changes and data usage and has no other way of easily obtain-

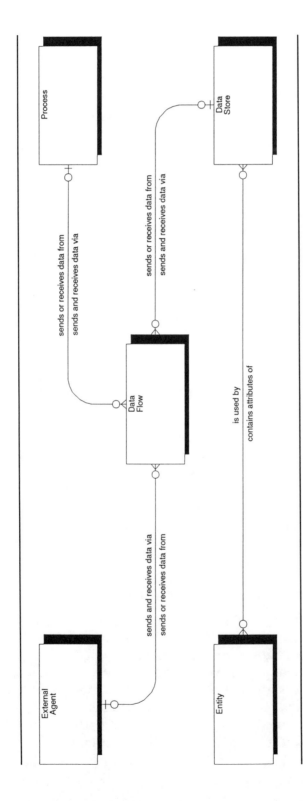

Figure 5.7. Entity Relationship Diagrammer : logical data process linkage.

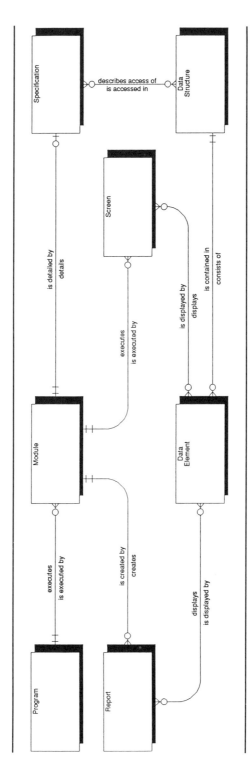

Figure 5.8. Entity Relationship Diagrammer : physical linkage information model.

117

ing this same information, it is likely worth the effort to manually make the change.

2. If so, between what objects?

Add relationships for each set of objects to be maintained in matrices. Examples are Entities and Processes, Attributes and Processes, Screens and Data Elements. Most relationships will be many-to-many, indicating that a row object can be used by multiple column objects and a column object can use multiple row objects.

3. Will an Entity Life Cycle Matrix be maintained?

If so, add as detailed properties of the relationship between entity and process the specific accesses you will track. Optionally, one relationship line could be added for each type of access.

4. Will dataflow diagrams be maintained?

As with matrices, dataflow diagrams can be valuable to the development and the maintenance teams. However, if automatic update is not facilitated by the CASE tool, long-term maintenance of the dataflow diagrams should be evaluated. If a change is made, such as a process or program name change, will the associated dataflow diagram also be changed? If not, manual effort will be required to make the change. If the diagram is used frequently, the information is not easily available elsewhere, and the dataflow cannot be generated from existing sources such as program code, manual maintenance may be justified.

If the dataflow diagrams are to be maintained, add the new objects that are on the dataflow diagram but do not already exist on the data or process information model. Examples include Data Stores, External Agents, and Data Flows.

5. What are the relationships between dataflow diagram objects?

First consider the relationship between the newly added objects. Can a data store directly reference an external agent? In most methodologies, this is not possible. Data Stores and External

Agents can only reference Data Flows. In these cases, add a one-to-many relationship between Data Stores and Data Flows and External Agents and Data Flows. This implies that a Data Store or External Agent can send data through or receive data from many Data Flows and a single dataflow sends data to or receives data from only one External Agent or Data Store.

If junctions are allowed in the methodology, the relationship may be changed to a many-to-many relationship, indicating that a Data Flow may relate to multiple Data Stores and/or External Agents. The relationship may also be changed to a many-to-many relationship if a single Data Flow name can be used in multiple dataflow diagrams or multiple times in the same diagram.

6. How is the Data Flow Diagram linked to the process model?

If dataflow diagrams are developed at a logical level, the logical process object, usually the Process, is directly used on the dataflow diagram itself. The relationship is similar to that between the Data Store or External Agent and the Data Flow. The Process may send information to or receive information from many Data Flows. If junctions apply or a dataflow name can be reused, a dataflow may be used by many different processes, indicating a many-to-many relationship. Otherwise, a one-to-many relationship from the Process to the Data Flow exists.

7. How is the Data Flow Diagram linked to the data model?

Add a relationship line for each technique employed to link the data model to the dataflow diagram. Possibilities include:

- A one-to-one relationship between the Entity and the Data Store, indicating that a Data Store equates to an Entity.
- A many-to-many relationship between the Entity and the Data Store or Data Flow, indicating that a Data Store or Data Flow can represent multiple Entities and an Entity can be represented by multiple Data Stores or Data Flows.
- A many-to-many relationship between the Entity and the Pro-

cess, indicating a Process can reference multiple Entities and an Entity may be used by multiple Processes.
* Similar relationships between the Process, Data Flow, or Data Store and the attribute.

8. What additional objects are used to represent physical linkage models?

If additional objects such as screen layouts or report layouts are used for linkage and were not added as a part of the process information model, they should be added at this time. In most cases, it is appropriate to add specifications as a separate object, although they can also be considered as detailed properties of the program or module. If versions of specifications are maintained, there is a one-to-many relationship between program or module and the specifications. Otherwise, there is a one-to-one relationship. For the purposes of modeling, the remaining questions will assume that a module specification object has been added. If not, replace references to module specification with module or program as applicable.

9. How are process objects referenced by the screens, reports, and specifications?

Specifications are linked to the program or module they describe in the previous question. In addition, they may call other programs or modules. This calling structure was established in the process information model. If the calling structure is actually established and maintained through the specification rather than another model, such as the structure chart, the relationship between the programs or modules may be modeled through the specification. A one-to-many relationship between the specification and modules indicates that the program or module implemented by the specification could call many modules. This relationship would be in addition to the standard relationship between the program or module and the specification that describes it.

Screens and reports may be linked to programs or modules through specifications or through direct relationships. If the screen or report linkage is tracked through the specification, add a one-to-one relationship if modules can create only one screen or report and a screen or report can be created by only one module. If a module can generate multiple screens or reports, the relationship is a one-to-many from the module to the screen or report. If a screen or report could be generated by multiple modules, as in the case of a standard audit report, the relationship is a many-to-many. The same principles apply to relationships directly with the program or module.

10. How are data objects referenced by screens, reports, and specifications?

Screens and reports generally reference specific data elements. In this case, relationships should be added between the screen or report and data element. Generally this is a many-to-many relationship since a screen or report has many data elements and a data element can appear on many screens or reports. If the physical portion of the data information model uses different objects to represent detailed pieces of information, such as fields and columns, the relationships should be added to these objects.

Specifications may detail processing logic at the data element level or at a higher level. The relationship should be added to one or the other using a many-to-many relationship since a specification can reference multiple data objects and a data object can be used by multiple specifications. If the higher-level data object is connected to the data element-level data object, both relationships are not needed since a relationship to a data element implies the relationship to the higher level.

In pure object-oriented environments, a module may support processing for one and only one group of data. In this case, a one-to-one or one-to-many relationship may apply between the physical data object and the specification or module. A close evaluation of the design techniques in use can highlight the correct relationship approach.

11. Where are potential areas of redundant linkages and properties?

As with the data and process information models, this total combined information model has the opportunity for redundant information. Look for places where relationship lines are added twice. For example, a relationship may have been added between a Process and Entity as a result of a matrix and a dataflow diagram. This indicates that the same information could be maintained in multiple ways. It may highlight that one of the models is not needed.

Duplicate properties are also a possibility. Consider the physical process objects. If definition was identified as a possible property, does this duplicate the specification? Does the screen layout contain data element formats that are also tracked in the database definition? If these areas of duplication represent different information, they may both be required. Otherwise, the detailed properties should be reevaluated to identify a single location for maintenance.

The approach outlined through these questions creates a basic information model, such as that shown in Figure 5.8. It is only one possible approach to information model development. An experienced data analyst in the organization can customize these questions and the resulting instructions to match the data analysis techniques in use by the organization. In this approach, no attempt was made to develop a fully normalized data model since the purpose was to identify basic business requirements. If the organization wishes to use the resulting model to build a repository structure, additional refinement may be required.

LINKAGE ACTIVITY MODELS

The activity model for linkage model management illustrates the major tasks performed in managing the linkage between data and process models. A sample activity model is displayed in Figure 5.9. This model divides activities into major groups based on the types of functions the model manager performs. Identifying objects, linkages, and associated standards is viewed as the first major function. Providing all necessary groups with access to the models is the second. The third functional grouping includes major tasks required to ensure the validity of the models.

Figure 5.10 illustrates an important part of linkage model validity checking. If changes are made to the data or process models, all appropriate changes must be made to the linkage

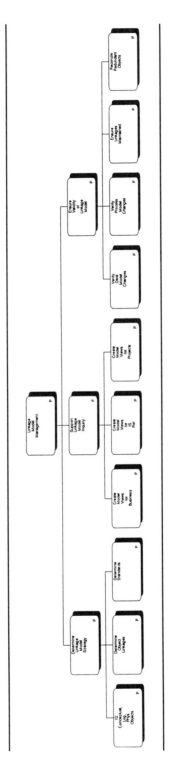

Figure 5.9. Decomposition Diagrammer : linkage model management.

123

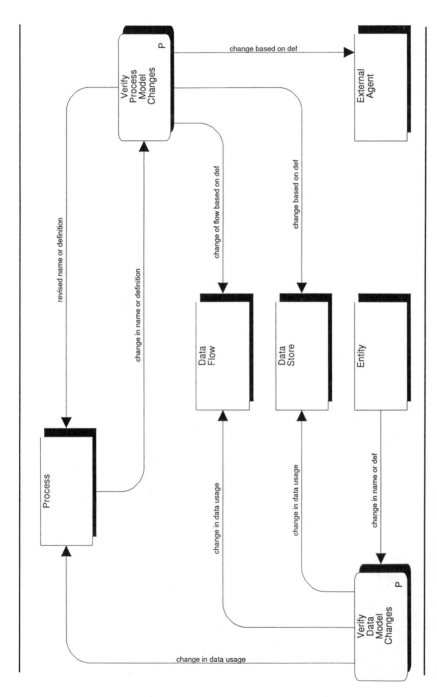

Figure 5.10. Data Flow Diagrammer : ensuring validity of linkage model.

model. The diagram focuses on the changes that may be required in a dataflow diagram as a result of a change. If an entity name or definition is changed, processes, dataflows, and data stores that reference the entity may require changes. If a process definition or name is changed, revisions may be required in the process itself, in other processes, in dataflows, in external agents, and in data stores. This type of diagram provides a type of checklist for the model manager.

Developing a Customized Linkage Activity Model

Just as each organization will have its own information model, it will also have its own activity model. The structure of the activity model will likely differ based on the way in which the organization assigns responsibility for model management activities. The specific tasks will also differ since each organization will have different priorities as well as different objects to be managed. The following questions have been designed to assist the organization in developing an initial process activity model. The emphasis at this stage should be on identifying the required tasks. In later chapters, options for organizing the model will be discussed.

1. Who will use the models?

The answer to this question will likely be the same audience who uses data and process models. Both Information Systems and business planners also have a distinct interest in linkage models since they illustrate how the business and systems use information. From an Information Systems standpoint, these models help identify critical data that is used by multiple applications. From a business standpoint, these models highlight areas of coordination across departments and individuals within departments.

2. When will they need access to the models?

As with data and process models, the need for immediate, on-request access places an emphasis on the need for strong procedures and automated facilities that provide efficient model access.

3. *How will changes to the data and process models be incorporated into the linkage models?*

The answer to this critical question depends a great deal on the CASE tools in use and how well they automatically support linkages. If little automated support is available, the model manager will need to evaluate carefully the benefit of the linkages compared to the manual effort required to maintain them.

4. *How will conceptual and logical models be verified?*

The same mechanisms identified for verification of data and process models will likely apply to linkage models.

5. *How will physical models be verified?*

Most physical models can be verified through program code. Physical screen maps may be available for verifying screen layouts. Any automated facilities that can assist in this verification will save a great deal of effort.

These are some of the major issues to be evaluated in developing the activity model. Each organization will identify activities specific to linkage model management as it gains experience in model development, usage, and management.

6

Project-Level Model Management

DEFINITION OF PROJECT MODEL MANAGEMENT

The most basic form of model management occurs within a project team. On a team with one individual, the developer is responsible for ensuring that all required objects are created and are linked appropriately to provide the information necessary for efficient, effective application development. However, when more than one individual is involved in the model development activities for the project, model management becomes a much more complex task. The work of all developers must be coordinated to ensure that the resulting models accurately combine to represent both the business and the systems that support it.

Critical issues in project-level model management include assigning responsibility for objects and linkages to the team members, coordinating the use of shared objects, and resolving conflicts within the model. It is also important to identify clearly for the team which objects and linkages are required. The team can then identify which diagrams and modeling techniques will best help them meet model management and project communication requirements.

STORAGE OF PROJECT MODELS

The types of CASE tools in use greatly affect the approach to project-level model management. If a tool resides in a centralized location such as a mainframe or network, where all analysts develop and maintain a single set of models, the model management issues focus on timing of changes to objects and responsibility for object creation and maintenance. If each analyst works on his or her own set of models on a separate workstation, the issue of sharing common objects across physically separate model repositories complicates the model management activities.

Single Project Repository

If a single repository is used by the team, all analysts are updating the same version of objects. A CASE tool operating in this environment usually has the capability of handling object locking to prevent concurrent update, but analysts still must time their activities. If two analysts had both planned to update the same specification at the same time, one would have to find an alternative activity.

The problem of timing activities is relatively minor compared to the underlying problem that causes timing conflicts. If two analysts are updating the same object, there is a potential for conflict. Suppose analyst A changes the length of Product Number from 6 to 9 positions after being notified of a change in the business definition of Product Number to include the specification of the division. Analyst B looked at his screen that used Product Number and noticed the change. Thinking it was an error, he changed it back to 6 positions. Meanwhile, analyst C heard about the same change and added a new data element, Division Code, which was 3 positions. At the next project status meeting, one week and fifteen screens and specifications later, the three analysts may realize the mistake, agree on a common solution, and then make the appropriate changes.

Effective model management could have avoided this problem before it happened. By either assigning a specific individual responsibility for making data changes and communicating changes to all team members or by instituting change notification procedures for shared objects, all analysts would have implemented a common change and would have understood the impact on existing objects that they supported.

Consider the situation of a project team using Knowledge-

Ware's ADW with a single-project encyclopedia. The team could be using the Analysis Workstation in group modeling sessions. If only one session occurred at a point in time, the analysts could take turns using the single-project encyclopedia to develop models. Any work that needed to occur after the sessions could be coordinated between the analysts through scheduling of the PC that contained the encyclopedia.

If a project team was utilizing KnowledgeWare's IEW/Mainframe product as the project CASE tool environment, the team could establish a single-project encyclopedia. The tool only allows an encyclopedia to be open for update by a single user. All other users can only read the encyclopedia while one user is using it for updating. If the majority of the team's efforts were performed outside the CASE tool, this could be a feasible approach. For example, the project team could hold JAD sessions where a single analyst was responsible for recording the results in the tool. Other team members could still access the models in the encyclopedia as reference.

If the mainframe- or PC-based tool with a single-project encyclopedia was also used during the design phase when several analysts were working on specifications, the single-project encyclopedia could be limiting since only one analyst could record information into the encyclopedia at a time. Single-project encyclopedias can also become a problem if project scheduling requires concurrent planning or analysis modeling sessions were needed.

Multiple-Project Repositories

If each analyst was working in his or her own repository on a separate workstation, the scenario of three analysts making conflicting changes may not have been caught until project implementation. At this level, it is difficult to identify common objects. For example, analyst A may be using a data element called Product Number. Analyst B may use Product Identifier. These may or may not represent the same object. They may even represent two different approaches to solving the same business problem. If the analysts are working separately, this situation would be difficult to detect.

In this type of environment, it is important to identify which objects and linkages are potentially common to all analysts and assign responsibility for managing those objects to a specific individual. Management in this context means coordinating all changes to the common object, keeping the master version of the common objects, and merging changed objects into other analysts' repositories so that they are working with the most up-to-date version possible.

This final activity of merging can be very time-consuming, especially with CASE tools that do not easily facilitate model combination. One possible approach is to merge all analyst repositories into one common repository at a specified interval, perhaps weekly. Then the common repository would be redistributed to all analysts. Two potential problems can arise in this approach. First, the model manager often is required to perform the merging at night or over the weekend to reduce the potential downtime of the analysts since they cannot be updating models while the merging is occurring. Secondly, it is difficult to determine which analyst has the correct set of changes to be redistributed to all analysts. If analyst A deleted a process from a diagram and analyst B renamed the deleted process, should the process be deleted from the project repository? This reconciliation activity for model discrepancies can be more time-consuming than the actual model-merging activity.

Instead of merging all analyst repositories, it is possible to identify those pieces that constitute shared objects or linkages. Only this information would be merged together at a common level and then re-merged into each analyst's repository. For example, if the data objects were identified as common, all data objects could be combined into a project repository weekly. Any reconciliation could then be performed on these objects and then the finalized data model would be merged with the existing models on each analyst's workstation. While this approach may reduce the time required for reconciliation and initial merging into a common repository, it will likely take more time at the end of the activity since the common repository will be merged with each individual analyst's existing models. This merging may take longer than the simple copy facilitated by the previous approach.

A project team could install the KnowledgeWare workstation

products on each analyst's personal computer. Each analyst could be assigned a portion of the project to develop on his or her own workstation. Shared information could be combined using a consolidation to each analyst's personal computer on a periodic basis. The key to the success of this approach is the ability to assign responsibility within the project team in a way that involves as little shared information as possible.

ASSIGNING RESPONSIBILITY WITHIN THE TEAM

Responsibility by Object Type

The easiest technique for assigning object maintenance responsibility is by object type. For example, a project data analyst could be responsible for all entities, attributes, relationships, and physical data structures. An application analyst may be responsible for logical process and linkage objects, such as processes, dataflows, and external agents. An application designer may be responsible for the detailed specifications and screen and report layouts.

An analysis project using KnowledgeWare's Analysis Workstation may assign one analyst the responsibility for developing and maintaining the entity model and the corresponding attributes and relationships. Another analyst may be responsible for developing the process models, using the Decomposition Diagrammer. A third analyst could develop dataflow diagrams, using both the data and process models developed by the other analysts. To avoid complex model management issues, the dataflow analyst could begin work after the other two analysts completed their analysis.

Responsibility by Logical Groups

In many projects, this ideal type of structure is not feasible since multiple analysts or designers need to be at work at the same time to complete the project in a realistic time frame. When multiple analysts need to work on the same type of object, it is easiest to split responsibility based on a group of related objects of the same object type.

In analysis, a process decomposition diagram could be used as the foundation for splitting responsibility. As shown in Figure 6.1,

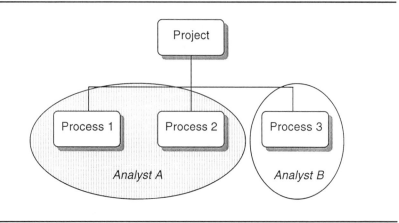

Figure 6.1.   Responsibility by Process Groupings.

a process model may be divided into several major groupings. By assigning analyst A responsibility for processes 1 and 2, and analyst B responsibility for process 3, each analyst can work relatively independently, decomposing processes, building dataflow diagrams, and beginning specifications.

Critical to the success of this approach is a clear definition of the processes at the level where responsibility is assigned. For example, suppose five main processes are identified as functions performed by the Marketing Planning department: Analyze Prior Sales, Determine Special Factors, Forecast Sales, Develop Marketing Plans, Monitor Sales. The activities of capturing sales history may occur as a part of Monitoring Sales or Analyzing Prior Sales. Without a definition of each of these processes, two analysts working independently may both detail the requirements for capturing sales. Not only is this duplicate work, it may result in two slightly different models that need to be reconciled. A more dangerous scenario may be the assumption on the part of each analyst that the other is documenting the sales collection process. This important set of activities with strong Information Systems implications may be overlooked in the scope of a large analysis project.

Since most analysts will likely overlap data usage, it is optimal to assign responsibility for data objects to a single individual so that data changes between multiple analysts can be easily coordinated. In this situation, all analysts requiring changes to the data model would request that the data analyst make the change. The data analyst would then analyze the change and determine the impact it would have on the data model and on other analysts. Changes would then be distributed to all analysts who use the data object (Figure 6.2). This puts the data analyst in a coordination role; therefore, the team skills of the analyst should be carefully reviewed prior to assigning data model responsibility.

Responsibility for data objects may seem to be a relatively straightforward assignment, but the scope should be considered. Does data include data stores on dataflow diagrams and references to data in specifications? Or is the data analyst only responsible for the entities, attributes, and relationships and simply making analysts aware of changes to these objects so the analysts themselves can change the dataflow diagrams and specifications? The decision depends on the ability of the analysts to correctly interpret the implications of a data change, the ability of the tool to automate some of the changes, and the ability of the data analyst to correctly change the linkage objects.

At the design level, a similar approach could be taken by assigning an analyst responsibility for a group of related screens, reports, or batch programs. The problem of clear definitions that exist at this level is identical to those faced in a non-model environment where two programmers may include similar logic in two programs. A coordination point may be helpful to look for areas of logic reuse.

A data designer, potentially the database analyst for the project, could be assigned responsibility for the physical data model (Figure 6.3). As in the case of the logical data analyst, the scope of the database analyst's change responsibility must be defined, especially if the CASE tool does not fully integrate the data objects and their use on layouts and in specifications. For example, if the length of Customer Address changes from 30 to 35 characters, does the database analyst have responsibility for changing all screen layouts to reflect the new size, or does he or she simply need to inform all designers of the change, and they are then responsible for making the change to the screens?

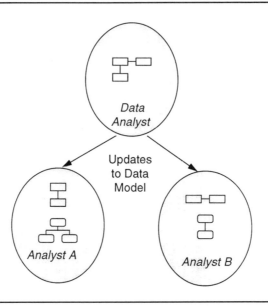

Figure 6.2.   Centralized Responsibility for Data.

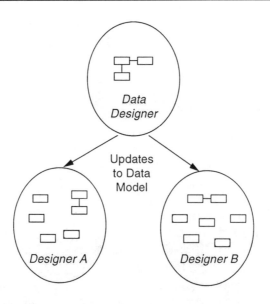

Figure 6.3.   Centralized Responsibility for Physical Data.

Throughout the life cycle, this focused approach has the advantage of allowing an analyst to focus on an area of the business and therefore provide better service to the specific group that will use the final system. From a data perspective, this approach better separates the different skills required for data and process modeling and helps reduce the tendency of new data modelers to introduce a process orientation to data models. However, it can be the foundation for struggles when responsibility is not clearly defined within the project team.

In the design phase of a project using KnowledgeWare's Design Workstation on personal computers, the Database Administrator may be assigned responsibility for maintaining the relations and relational database. If standards and procedures require that screen layouts are built using the data structures defined by the relations, most maintenance to relations will automatically be reflected in the screen layout. A simple change control procedure could also be implemented where the Database Administrator informed all analysts of any database changes through weekly update memos. The developers could each be assigned a set of modules to develop specifications for, based on the system structure chart. One developer could be assigned responsibility for maintaining all common modules that could be used by all analysts. The model manager would assist the Database Administrator and the common module developer in merging their changes into the models developed by the other developers.

Joint Update of Objects

In some cases, the division based on logical groupings is not practical. For example, if analysts on the project team have different skill sets, the best use of project resources may require multiple analysts to work on the same objects. Just as it is difficult to have two programmers modifying the same program at the same time, coordination is difficult in model development.

One analyst may be strong in developing an overall, high-level view of the system, while another is stronger at developing efficient, effective detailed specifications for a CICS environment. The first analyst may have responsibility for identifying the need for a program and writing high-level specifications, while the second analyst may refine those specifications.

If the CASE tool in use does not have separate objects for high-level and detailed specifications, the two analysts may be maintaining the same object. If the two analysts are working on a network- or mainframe-based CASE tool, the critical issue becomes one of timing changes. If separate workstations containing separate repositories are used, coordination of objects between the two may require frequent merging of repositories. For this reason, the duplicate responsibility approach is more applicable to a network or mainframe environment than to an individual workstation setup.

Making this approach work in a multiple-repository environment may require strict procedures used by the analysts. On a daily basis, they might agree on which specifications each will work on, avoiding any duplication of work. At the beginning of each day, each analyst would either create a mini-repository, containing only those objects they needed to work on, or would get a copy of the entire repository. At the end of the day, the analyst would merge any changed objects back to a common repository.

If, for some reason, two analysts needed to work on the same object, they would first need to review limitations of the CASE tool. If it would not merge the details of the objects, they may need to allow one person to work on the object, copy its contents to the other analyst's repository, and then let the second analyst complete his or her work. If the CASE tool does allow true merges, the rules of the merge would need to be reviewed to ensure that all work done by each analyst would be retained. Even in this situation, the sequence of the merges may need to be planned carefully to ensure that the correct result is achieved.

In a scenario such as this, the project team either needs a full-time project model manager or needs to become extremely proficient in model management techniques itself. A portion of the day in the morning and late afternoon will probably be consumed in model management activities while heavy maintenance is underway on commonly maintained objects.

Suppose a project team is selected to perform analysis on a business area using KnowledgeWare's Analysis Workstation. One analyst is an experienced dataflow diagrammer. Another is a beginning modeler and is uncomfortable with most modeling techniques. The inexperienced analyst is therefore assigned responsibility for developing process models, one of the easiest models to develop. To avoid a delay in the experienced analyst's efforts, the two decide to work simultaneously. Each evening, the process model analyst creates a consolidation file of the new processes developed that day and any changes made to existing processes. Each morning, the dataflow diagram analyst consolidates those changes onto her personal computer, begins development of dataflow diagrams for the new processes, and reviews the changed processes for potential dataflow diagram changes. Any deletions or name changes are manually tracked by the process model developer and given to the dataflow diagram developer with each consolidation file since the release of the Analysis Workstation does not have a mechanism for tracking these types of changes.

COORDINATING USE OF SHARED OBJECTS

Even with a clear definition of object and linkage creation and maintenance responsibility, there is still a need to coordinate the use of these shared objects throughout the team. This involves two types of activities. Model management must ensure that when an object is changed, all references to the object are also changed. In addition, all references must use the object consistently.

Ensuring model integrity implies that changes will be correctly reflected in the model. If the name of a data element is changed, the change must be reflected in all places where the data element is referenced. If the name of a process changes, it must be changed in both the process model and the associated dataflow diagram.

For organizations using CASE tools that use the same object instance in all models, this change is automatically facilitated by the initial change. However, suppose the organization has set a standard that data stores represent one and only one entity. If the entity name is changed, the data store name may not be automatically changed if the tool does not enforce the same requirements as the organization. It is important to understand which rules are automatically enforced and which must be manually enforced through standards and procedures.

Model consistency is perhaps more difficult to achieve. It requires that a model manager understand each usage of an object to ensure that all uses are consistent. An analyst may use the entity ITEM to refer to a product that is manufactured by the firm. Another analyst on the same project may interpret the entity ITEM to mean a product purchased from an outside vendor. Both of those interpretations may be valid, based on the definition of ITEM. However, if the ITEM entity only includes manufactured products, one of the analyst's references to ITEM is incorrect. Perhaps a new entity, PURCHASED ITEM, is needed to fulfill the needs of the second analyst. Clear communication and model review may have highlighted this error very early in the analysis process, before any design or construction activities have occurred.

RESOLVING MODEL CONFLICTS

For shared objects and linkages, conflicts are inevitable. Analyst A would like to use the data element Product Number. His users already have a preprinted form that uses this term. Analyst B prefers Product Identifier, which is correct according to naming standards since it can be alphanumeric and the term Number is reserved for numeric fields. The model manager is put in a no-win situation. She has been told by management that standards must be enforced, while knowing that the user's preferred terminology should be used whenever possible.

Decisions such as this confront the project model manager daily. Standards can help resolve many of these easily. However, in cases where there seem to be valid reasons to bend standards, or where the standards are not sufficiently clear to apply to the specific situation, several other factors can be used to assist in reconciliation.

One of the best means of conflict resolution is to refer to existing models. If several other projects have used the term Product Number, the model manager can use these as a precedent and use the term preferred by the user. Unfortunately, precedents sometimes conflict with the instincts of the model manager and other reasons are needed.

Individuals within the business can be strong supporters of model management decisions. Often if the model manager explains options, the business can help the manager assess the impact to other models in other parts of the business. This nontechnical viewpoint can be critical in evaluating all possible solutions.

Future directions within the business and Information Systems groups should also be considered when resolving model conflicts. A decision may apply today, but may be in conflict with the direction the business is moving in. Knowledge of planned models also helps the model manager assess the impact of a decision. If several more models are planned in the area, a decision may be much more important since it could affect the future models.

Another possible approach is to analyze the potential impact of the change to existing models in the project. Suppose Product Identifier is used in 12 places but Product Number is only referenced in 5. It is easier to change all references of Product Number to Product Identifier than vice versa.

Project model managers must always be cautious when making decisions to deviate from standards. Allowing a nonstandard format may seen minor to the design team, but it may not be supported by the target database environment. A minor change in module-naming standards may cause problems with existing security facilities. Although a problem may not be evident in this project, it may occur for a later project. Consider a project that elects to use data element groups because they are not targeting a relational database environment. If the resulting data structure is later migrated to a relational database, major changes may be required. Model managers should carefully review all potential implications and evaluate the consequences, even if it means requiring the team to deviate from the direction requested by the business.

THE PROJECT INFORMATION MODEL

The project information model represents the relationships between objects developed during the project development life cycle. It should include all the relationships that the project team is responsible for creating and preserving. It may not represent the long-term objects that are maintained on a corporate-wide level after project implementation.

For example, during development it may be important for dataflow diagrams to be fully developed and maintained to assist in the accurate design of the application. However, once the application is installed, the firm may decide that continued maintenance of detailed dataflow diagrams does not provide a benefit that justifies the cost of the maintenance resources. Yet it is important to ensure that the project information model accurately reflects the requirement of detailed dataflow diagrams so that the team understands expected deliverables and their relationships.

The project information model may also differ by project. A team that analyzes the business and creates a high-level system design, which is implemented in an expert system outside the CASE tool arena, may only create the logical portions of the information model. A project that is building a common repository of critical data for use by subsequent projects, such as an Employee Database, may develop only data portions of the model. The project team, the business, and the corporate model managers must understand the specific portions of the model that are to be developed, and a project information model is an ideal approach to clear documentation of deliverables.

THE PROJECT ACTIVITY MODEL

In developing the project activity model, many of the same activities identified in Chapters 3, 4 and 5 will be required. The project model may be somewhat smaller in scope since some of the activities were specific to management of objects across projects. It may be helpful to organize the project activity model based on the project life cycle. This clearly identifies the procedures that will be followed at each phase by the team members. The model should clearly identify responsibility for those procedures within the team.

In addition to the questions used to develop activity models for specific types of models, project model managers supporting multiple project repositories should address the following questions:

1. What objects and linkages should be merged so that models can be shared across the project?

This critical identification of common objects and linkages can help ensure model integrity throughout the project life cycle. By developing and maintaining valid models at the project level, the corporate model management tasks are reduced. This identification should be determined prior to the beginning of each phase so that models can be readily available.

2. When should the merges occur?

If merges are identified but performed too late, the merge is useless to the analyst, who may have already developed his or her own version of the common model to meet needs. Merges can either be performed at a set time—for example, weekly—or after a major set of changes has occurred. The timing will depend on how the models are structured, how often changes are made, and how time-consuming the merges are to perform.

3. How will be merges be performed?

If the CASE tools in use provide facilities for merging, the major decision is who will be responsible for executing and validating the merges. If little automation is available, especially in the identification of redundant objects, a complete set of procedures may need to be developed.

7

Corporate-Wide Model Management

DEFINITION OF CORPORATE MODEL MANAGEMENT

Corporate model management involves many of the same issues addressed in project model management, but on a much larger scale. Instead of coordinating between multiple analysts, the model manager must now coordinate multiple analysts working on multiple projects.

In an environment where integrated databases and shareable modules are not applicable, corporate-wide model management may be as simple as combining models from highly related projects. For example, a set of models may exist for the Finance area. If all Finance programs are maintained by the same group and used only within Finance applications, and if all data structures are used only by the Finance applications, changes made to the Finance models will have no impact on other models. The only concern would be managing the timing of project model implementation. If Finance project 2 were to be installed after Finance project 1, model management would ensure that all changes made by project 1 to objects also used by project 2 were incorporated into project 2 models. In this simplistic environment, model management can be a function of one of the application development team members since coordination with other teams is not required.

However, as many organizations move toward a more integrative environment, the issues of model management become much more complex. For example, suppose a manufacturing project is scheduled for implementation in July. A new forecasting system and an inventory control system are both scheduled for early September implementation. The manufacturing project and the forecasting project have both modified the same set of product data. The Inventory Control project assumed it could use several of the modules developed by Manufacturing and used their specification models. If the manufacturing project slips by three months, two projects in two different areas are affected. The base product data assumed by Forecasting and the base process model used by Inventory Control are now incorrect. The manufacturing project models are also incorrect since they do not include changes made in the other two projects. Therefore, tracking model usage across projects and coordinating changes becomes a critical issue for the model manager.

DEFINING THE CORPORATE MODEL

The first step in corporate-wide model management is the definition of corporate to the organization. In some small organizations, corporate may mean all departments within the organization. However, to larger corporations, corporate may mean a specific division within the organization. If no need exists to control information or activities across divisions except for consolidated financial reporting, then divisional-based corporate repositories may be sufficient. Divisional repositories are especially applicable if each division has its own information services function and there are limited shared departments.

From a modeling perspective, the definition of corporate models is also concerned with the amount of interaction required among the models from different groups. Although the Finance department may send information to and receive information from the Marketing department, the single interface between the two may be represented by a file or set of reports that are exchanged. Each department may have its own dedicated Information Systems support group, with its own set of standards, procedures, and modeling activities. Shared data is limited to the confines of a department. In this case, the definition of corporate models would be at the department level.

LEVELS OF CORPORATE MODELS

Once corporate is identified for the organization, the next step is to identify which models actually constitute corporate-level models. Some models or specific objects within models may not be required at a corporate level. Some may be required only during the application development process and may not be needed once the project has reached maintenance activities. Some model information may be needed by the maintenance team but may not be needed by other individuals in the organization.

In some organizations, one single corporate repository of models could exist. All models developed by all projects would be housed in this single location. Although it is easier to retrieve models from this environment, model maintenance can be a nightmare. A single change to a common module used by many applications, such as a date conversion module, may change the resulting programs for many applications. If the change is correct and is truly intended for all programs, this situation would be an easy way to approach mass change. However, this may not be the case in all environments.

If the organization is not yet in a position to have totally integrated models across all applications, there are options to still achieving some of the benefits of shared models. It is likely that the organization does have some areas where a centralized repository is desirable. For example, a common set of subroutines may already be in use. These may be an excellent starting point for the corporate-wide repository. Data may already be uniquely defined across projects, especially in specific commonly used areas, such as Product and Customer. These shared data objects could also be placed in the corporate repository.

Model objects that are not unique at this time across all projects could still be combined to achieve some type of commonality. Perhaps all models in the Manufacturing area are unique. Then all project models that affect Manufacturing could be merged together. This would create another level of repository between the project level and the corporate level. In this case, the intermediate level would be an application level containing all models for Manufacturing applications.

This application-level approach is particularly applicable to organizations that structure their Information Systems staff based on department or business-area groupings. One team of application developers may support the Finance department, another may support the Marketing department, and a third may support the Manufacturing department (Figure 7.1). In these organizations, the Information Systems groups tend to duplicate the structure of the organization itself. Generally they include an overall support group, including Database Administration and CASE tool support, that serves all teams.

Although grouping based on Information Systems staff structure may be appealing for many organizations, it can also be a major limitation in the future. If the organization reorganizes, the structure of the repositories may also need to be reorganized. For example, suppose Finance and Human Resources were established as two repositories. Payroll might originally fall as a part of the Finance area and be contained in the Finance repository. A reorganization could shift Payroll responsibility to the Human Resources department. If the change is also made in the

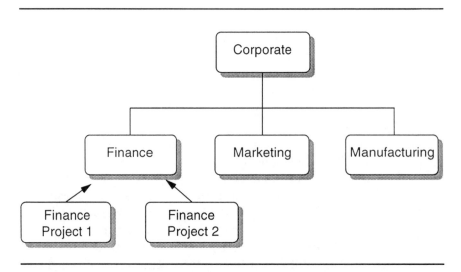

Figure 7.1.   Corporate Models with Applications Levels.

repositories, the model manager may have difficulty determining and isolating Payroll objects, and then encounter merging problems when the models are combined into the Human Resources repository.

Using the Payroll responsibility example above, suppose the Finance repository included basic Payroll models as well as electronic data interchange models for data transfer with the bank that paid the payroll and performed other corporate banking functions. The model manager would have to either duplicate the EDI model or ensure that documentation of the relationship was included in both repositories. When merging to the Human Resources repository, the model manager may find that HR and Payroll have basic differences in terminology. Something as basic as employee may have a different meaning in the two groups. To merge the models correctly, distinctions between HR employees and Payroll employees may be required. Grouping project models by application areas may encounter problems when projects are not clearly defined within a specific business area. Increasingly, cross-department projects are being undertaken. A new sales reporting system may be used by the Finance, Marketing and Inventory Control departments. Such a system might use processes and data from all three areas. If each department currently is represented by one applications area, several alternatives exist for long-term storage of the resulting models. A new application area may be identified, the project models may be split into three components stored separately, or the models may be stored redundantly in all three application areas.

Some environments may be able to combine models to a higher level than application, but may not be able to achieve a single corporate-level repository. Organizations can define business areas, which represent business-based groupings of applications. For example, General Ledger, Accounts Payable, and Payroll may all represent applications that support the Finance area. All models that support these three applications may be sufficiently unique to combine into a single Finance Business Area repository. This would be desirable if there were shared objects, such as the ledger file, used by all three applications and there were no conflicts between model objects and linkages in the application models.

Some Information Systems departments are organized based on job responsibility, rather than on applications support area. For example, there may be a group of planners that identifies future directions, including potential projects, for the Information Systems department. A team of business analysts performs all analysis activities for the potential projects. A group of application designers may then be responsible for developing and implementing a system that efficiently supports the requirements identified by the analysts. In this organizational structure, application-based repositories may not be appropriate. Instead, functional-based repositories may be used. A conceptual repository could house the conceptual models, a logical repository could house the logical models, and a physical repository could house the details of the actual system (Figure 7.2). This breakdown would only be appropriate if the organization did not need to track the linkages between the conceptual, logical, and physical data or process models. Any information that was needed by all three groups could be stored in a corporate-level repository.

As object-oriented development becomes more common, a subject-area approach to intermediate repositories may be applicable. In an object-oriented environment, definitions, rules, and

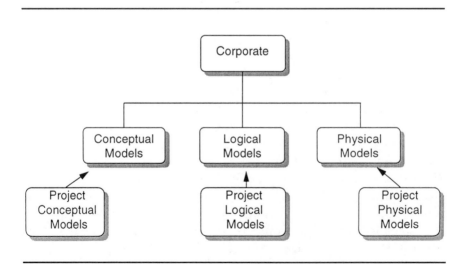

Figure 7.2.   Corporate Models with Functional Levels.

actions are centered around objects. For example, the rules for creating, modifying, and deleting a product may be stored with the Product data structure, instead of in a separate program that references the Product data structure. In this more data-driven environment, models may be grouped together based on logical data groupings, or subject areas. All information about Customer-related objects, such as Customer Demographics, Customer Sales History, and Customer Special Pricing, may be stored in the Customer Subject Area. Some organizations that are structuring their activities based on the concept of subject databases can take advantage of this structure without implementing true object-oriented approaches.

BUILDING THE CORPORATE INFORMATION MODEL

The corporate information model identifies the objects and linkages the organization is concerned about maintaining in the long run. This may differ from the project information model since there may be some objects or linkages that are necessary for the application development process but are not required for maintenance, new development, or end-user computing activities. For example, the conceptual model may be developed as a starting point for the logical model, but may not be maintained since the logical model includes all the components of the conceptual model but at a more detailed level. Organizations that do not need the higher-level model for further planning purposes may elect not to maintain it at the corporate level.

In analyzing the corporate information model, shared objects need to be placed at the highest level required. If data models are shared by all projects, they need to be placed at the corporate level. If screens are used only by specific applications, screen objects might be maintained at the application level. Information models are needed at all applicable levels so model managers and model users can easily identify the location of required model information.

Analyzing linkage requirements is more complex. Does it matter to the organization that the Product Entity is used by over 100 processes in 5 business area repositories? Or is the organization only concerned with the 100 programs that access the Product

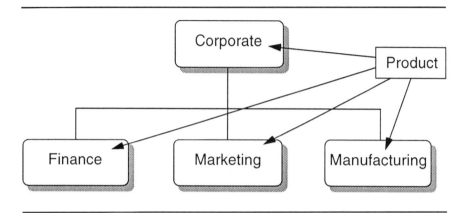

Figure 7.3.   Corporate Models with Redundant Objects.

Master File data structure? From a maintenance perspective, only the second situation may be required. However, the logical linkage may be needed to aid in communication with and among the business community.

If all objects with required linkages are maintained at the same level, maintaining the linkages is a natural part of model maintenance. However, suppose the Product Entity is stored in a corporate-level repository and processes are maintained at the business-area level. Unless the CASE tool allows a linkage to be stored without the two linked objects being stored in the same repository, the Product Entity object must be maintained redundantly at the business-area level (Figure 7.3). Since any introduction of redundant data risks discrepancies, careful procedures need to be established to ensure that duplicate objects in both repositories are identical.

CREATING PROJECT MODELS FROM CORPORATE MODELS

To increase the productivity gain resulting from the use of models with CASE tools, the models need to be available for reuse in other projects. A business process model may be developed for an entire business area. One initial project may have focused on a subset of this model. A subsequent project in the same area may be able to use the same business process model to gain an understanding of the business and then build from that model, saving the time of redeveloping a process model. At a more physical level, a project may have developed a set of routines, such as date conversion routines, that may be applicable to many other projects.

Facilitating this reuse involves the process of creating initial project models from existing corporate-level models. This requires accurate identification of the scope of the project from the project team and an understanding of the available models on the part of the corporate model manager. Often this is a continual updating process throughout the project life cycle since it is rare that a project team sufficiently understands its project during the planning phase to assist the model manager in selecting all appropriate objects and linkages. A phased approach may help alleviate some of the updates by selecting those objects and linkages appropriate to the phase the team is beginning. It is easier to identify the correct business area than to identify the correct common modules at the beginning of the analysis phase. At the design phase, the team is in a better position to identify potential common modules that can assist in the development process.

The importance of continually creating project models from the corporate model is best understood by a common scenario. A small project team was creating a four-file reporting database that could be linked to several high-use files, including the Price file and the Vendor file. An entity model was developed. Due to the small scope of the project, the team decided not to bother the corporate model manager and created their own entities for Price and Vendor, naming them 'Product Price' and ' Vendor', with a space accidently placed before Vendor. Upon project completion, the corporate model manager merged the small project model and missed the two incorrectly named entities. Now two additional entities existed in the corporate model. A later project needed to use the Price and Vendor entities. The corporate model manager selected the extra entities, still not recognizing the discrepancies. This later project was on a much larger scale and included many relationships using these entities. It may take several more projects for a problem such as this to be detected and then a great deal of effort to correct the corporate data model. In the meantime, vital information about data usage is incorrectly represented in what should be the most accurate source of data information, the corporate data model.

Suppose a project team is beginning the analysis phase of a new project. During the planning phase, the team identified several integration points with existing systems. The organization has implemented KnowledgeWare's Mainframe product as the storage location for the single, corporate encyclopedia. A consolidation file could be built with the interface entities, attributes, and relationships. A subject area could be created containing these objects with a name that identified the project. These could be given to the project team through a consolidation file to use as a starting point for the team's data model. As additional interface points were identified, the model manager could add the appropriate entities to the subject area and create a new consolidation file. This new consolidation file would be consolidated into the project team's data encyclopedia. As the team moved into design, the appropriate physical data structures could be added to the project team's data encyclopedia.

CHANGE MANAGEMENT FOR MODELS

Allowing a model to be used and potentially changed by another project brings its own set of problems for the model manager. If a model is changed, the manager must help the project team evaluate the impact of that change on other models. Different types of changes may have different degrees of impact. For example, a name change to one high-level process in a business process model will have little, if any, effect on existing models that reference that process. However, a name change to a data element that is used in over twenty specifications, ten screen layouts, and five report layouts would have significant impact on other models, especially in a code generation environment.

Change management for model managers involves tracking what changes are made and determining the required change to other models. Often the model developers are needed to correctly evaluate and complete any required changes to other models. Adding a new level to a primary key for a data structure may require that all developers of screens that use the key update the screen layout to include the new key level, as well as possibly update the corresponding specification. The model manager cannot correctly assess whether these types of business requirements changes are required, but he or she can identify that the potential exists and inform the correct individuals.

If multiple projects can be updating the same model concurrently, another level of complexity is added to the change management process. The model manager must keep track of all changes that are being made and inform other project teams of the changes that could potentially affect their development project. If each project uses its own repository or multiple workstation-based repositories, this can be a difficult task. An automated or manual tracking system of which project is using which object can be vital in assisting the model manager in this effort.

In the previous example, a subject area was established to identify a group of entities that were in use by a project team. To track usage simply, the model manager could consistently implement this subject area approach for all existing entities in project encyclopedias. To manage a change to an existing entity, the model manager could create an Object Summary report on the entity in the corporate model to obtain a list of all subject areas that used the entity. The model manager could then check with each project team to assess the impact of the change based on the project implementation date and its use of the entity.

UPDATING THE CORPORATE MODELS

Once the project is complete, the model manager must merge the project model into the corporate model. The actual merge process is the smallest of these activities. The effort comes from identifying the potential changes to existing models and then incorporating those changes where appropriate. An official change approval process can assist the model manager in this effort.

Suppose project A wishes to change a specification for a common module, used in many completed applications and several development projects. The model manager would help facilitate a discussion among all involved developers to assess the accuracy and impact of the change. If the accuracy is questionable or the impact is too great at this time, the model manager needs to be in a position to deny the change. If the team waits to inform the model manager of these changes until system implementation time, an implementation delay may be required. Therefore, helping the team track shared objects and providing an early mechanism for change approval can save both the project team and the model manager a great deal of anguish.

A project team has completed its analysis phase and wants to make its models available for use by other teams. The model manager reviews the changes and discovers that part of the model is a revision to an existing data model. The remainder is new analysis models. The model manager reviews the changed data pieces to verify that they are not used by another project. One entity is in use by a project planned for implementation after the team completing the analysis phase, so they are given a copy of the revised entity. The project team's analysis model is then consolidated into the corporate model using a combine option.

SUPPORTING NEW SOFTWARE RELEASES

Periodically, software vendors issue a new software release that changes the structure of the underlying CASE tool information model. For example, in KnowledgeWare's Release 2.7, Information Types replaces Data Types in the Analysis Workstation. Model managers need to be involved in such a change in two areas. First, they must evaluate the new features available to the organization and determine which ones make sense for their implementation. Second, they must determine how to convert existing corporate models to the new structure.

If the model manager has developed an information model for the current version of the CASE tool, planning the migration to the new release can be greatly facilitated. The manager can begin the evaluation by modeling the new structure provided by the vendor. If multiple CASE tools are used, this process may be complex since one may change, but the other tool will probably not be affected at the same time. A new information model for the organization can then be developed by evaluating which portions of the vendor's new model can be implemented by the organization.

For example, suppose the organization had implemented the data portions of KnowledgeWare's Analysis and Design Work-

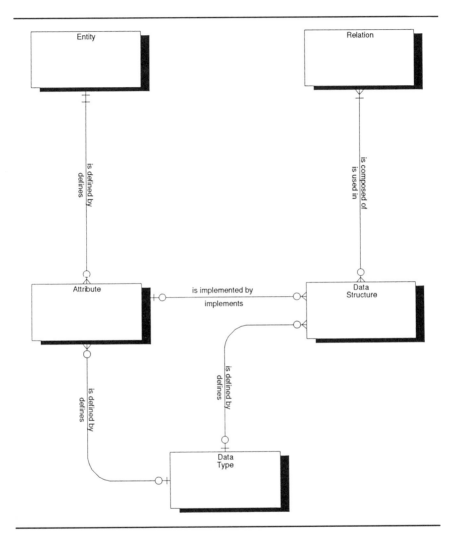

Figure 7.4.   Entity Relationship Diagrammer : Information Model 1.6.

stations as illustrated in Figure 7.4. After evaluating the options available under release 2.7, a new model was developed showing the use of Information Types and Catalog Entities, Attributes, and Relationships (Figure 7.5). The organization may decide to modify this diagram, showing that local data structures are not allowed in the organization (Figure 7.6).

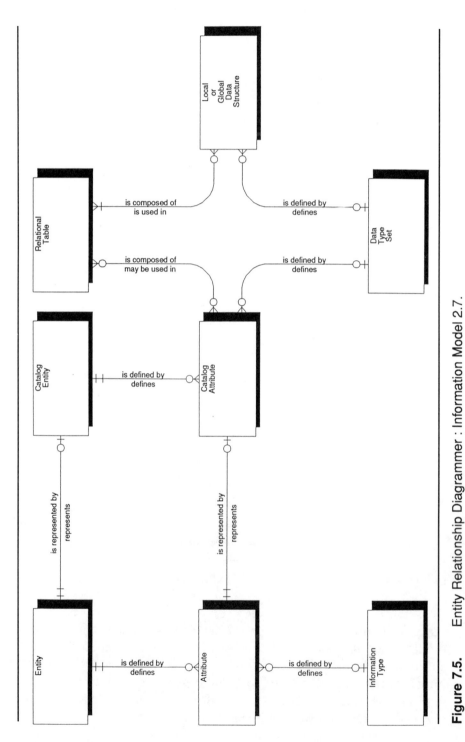

Figure 7.5. Entity Relationship Diagrammer : Information Model 2.7.

156

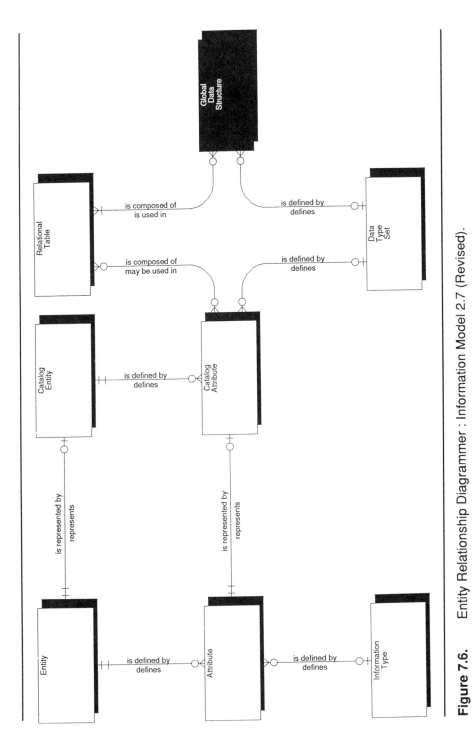

Figure 7.6. Entity Relationship Diagrammer : Information Model 2.7 (Revised).

Once the new information model is developed, the model manager should review the conversion utilities provided by the vendor. KnowledgeWare automatically converts encyclopedias from one version to another using the Reorganize facility. In the above scenario, KnowledgeWare could convert Local Data Types used in the Analysis Workstation to Information Types based on matching formats and Global Data Types directly to one Information Type. Therefore, if Price Amount and Product Weight had the same format and were assigned Local Data Types, they would be assigned the same Information Type. If the organization wanted an Information Type to encompass both the format and editing criteria, the migration strategy the model manager may implement could involve first creating global data types where local data types are now used and then executing the Reorganize facility.

BUILDING THE CORPORATE ACTIVITY MODEL

In developing the activity model at the corporate level, the model manager should address many of these issues. Specifically, the following areas should be considered:

1. *When should project models be merged to the corporate level?*

An easy solution is to merge completed models to the corporate level when the entire project is complete. However, for long projects, this may mean that work that the team completed in the analysis phase may not be available to other teams for more than a year. Intermediate merges may be established to provide better access to the project models. Model managers should be aware of the risk that these intermediate models may be changed by the project team and should be in a position to track users of these intermediate models and merge model changes as required.

A possible approach to identifying the intermediate merge points is to review the methodology and track how deliverables are referenced and modified. If the methodology includes several phases, all completed project models may be merged at the end of each phase. However, if many projects are occurring at a point in time, merging of all project models at the end of each phase may prove too labor-intensive. Instead, only those models that could be used by other teams and are relatively stable would be considered as candidates for intermediate corporate merges. For example, logical data models may be merged at the completion of the analysis phase. Physical data models, although completed during the design phase, may not be merged if they are likely to change significantly during a brief construction phase. High-level specifications completed during the analysis phase may not be merged since they are likely to change and would provide minimal benefits to other project teams.

2. How will integrity be ensured?

This question was originally raised at the data, process, and linkage model levels. At a corporate level, it is critical that mechanisms be established to ensure conceptual, logical, and physical model integrity for all models that will be reused. The scope of the integrity checks may be limited at the corporate-level to ensuring compliance with corporate level standards. It would be difficult for a model manager to assess accurately the business validity of logical models. Instead, the project teams may have responsibility for ensuring this more subjective type of integrity.

3. How will changes by projects be tracked?

Change management is a critical issue for model managers. The activity model should include procedures designed to assist in this process. This may be as simple as a spreadsheet that tracks existing models in use by project teams or may be an automated model tracking facility provided by a CASE tool vendor. Critical areas to be tracked are additions, deletions, and terminology changes that may affect the model manager's ability to merge completed models accurately.

If the model manager cannot be involved with project teams at a sufficiently detailed level to allow visibility of changes as they occur, it is possible to have the team track such changes and review them with the model manager at periodic update meetings. It is not advisable for the model manager to wait until the project is completed and then compare the new model with existing corporate models. Even if the CASE tool includes facilities to recognize name changes, the model manager may not correctly interpret the difference between a name change and the need for a new object. Incorrect models at this stage are usually left uncorrected by the project team, which has no real incentive to conform to standards after project completion, or are corrected by the model manager.

4. How will discrepancies be resolved?

A formal set of procedures for resolving conflicts is highly recommended. The more highly interrelated the models are, the more the model manager will be forced to deal with model conflict. By having established, understood procedures, this task can be streamlined.

Suppose project A wishes to change all references of Customer to Consumer. The business has requested this change and feels it more accurately reflects the current business direction. Several other projects may be using Customer-related models and may feel the change will negatively affect their business partners, who are accustomed to using the term Customer. The model manager should have a formal mechanism for project team A to request the change and then another mechanism that allows all affected project teams to meet together to discuss the change. In a situation such as this, a simple democratic vote will probably be unacceptable to project team A. Formal change review criteria need to be established, and an individual or set of individuals with sufficient authority needs to be appointed to make the final determination.

8

Developing a Model Management Strategy

WHY A CUSTOMIZED MODEL MANAGEMENT STRATEGY?

Even if each Information Systems organization was structured identically, used the same methodology, implemented the same set of CASE tools, and hired the identical set of Information Systems professionals, a single model management approach could not be recommended for implementation at every organization. Information Systems groups function within unique businesses and thus have different priorities. They also have their own sets of existing hardware and software that present different challenges to be met by model management. With so many different factors in place at each organization, a customized approach to model management is necessitated.

The following steps are designed to assist organizations in determining a model management direction and analyzing the impact of various alternatives. Additional considerations that are unique to the organization will likely surface during the analysis process. Once the framework has been determined, the detailed standards and procedures will need to be added.

The following two chapters will assist in identifying the appropriate individuals within the organization to assist in the actual implementation of the strategy and in the continuous improvement of the selected approaches.

STEP 1: IDENTIFY THE OBJECTS TO BE USED

The first step in developing a model management strategy is to identify the specific objects used in modeling. If an information model has been developed using the procedures outlined in Chapters 3, 4 and 5, the objects are all the objects illustrated in this model.

If an information model has not been developed, the list of objects can be derived by looking at the organization's methodology and developing a list of deliverables. Many of these deliverables will likely be produced by one or more of the CASE tools. Once the specific types of models are identified, research into the CASE tools in use can identify the specific objects the organization is using. The columns in Figure 8.1 represent a sample list of objects.

In the absence of a standard methodology, the model management team can develop this list by gathering samples of models produced by different projects. For model management to be successful, standards should be in place that can be implemented across projects. Therefore, the team should work with the project

	Attribute	Data Element	Data Flow	Data Group	Data Structure	Entity	Entity Relationship	Process	Program Specifications
Conceptual Data Objects				✓		✓			
Conceptual Process Objects								✓	
Logical Data Objects	✓			✓		✓	✓		
Logical Process Objects								✓	
Physical Data Objects		✓		✓					
Physical Process Objects									✓
Conceptual Data-Process Link									
Logical Data-Process Link			✓						
Physical Data-Process Link									✓
Conceptual-Logical Data Link				✓					
Conceptual-Logical Process Link								✓	
Logical-Physical Data Link	✓	✓				✓	✓		
Logical-Physical Process Link								✓	✓

Figure 8.1.   Association Matrix Diagrammer : object usage matrix.

groups and the business community to determine which of the models are most valuable and should be instituted as corporate standards. In areas where corporate-wide agreement cannot be reached, the models should be identified as noncorporate-wide models.

Although different groups may elect to display models differently, if the same basic objects are used the models can be assumed to be identical for management purposes. For example, project team A may prefer Chen notation on its entity relationship diagrams while team B may prefer Bachman notation. If both groups capture entities, relationships, and basic cardinalities, they are dealing with the same objects from a management perspective.

Once the objects have been identified, it is important to analyze how the objects are actually used by the organization. A matrix such as the one shown in Figure 8.1 is a good starting point for the analysis. The goal in this matrix is to identify objects that have dual usage, to highlight potential redundant objects, and to map the object to the appropriate model management concepts discussed in Chapters 3, 4 and 5.

Figure 8.1 illustrates several potential problem areas for model management. Entities, Processes, and Data Groups are all used for conceptual and logical modeling. This means that if maintenance of conceptual models is required, strict standards need to be developed to distinguish between conceptual and logical objects. More than one check in a column identifies potential redundant objects. For example, both Data Groups and Entities are used as conceptual data objects. Each of these objects needs to be carefully defined so that project teams understand which one to use in specific situations.

STEP 2: IDENTIFY REQUIRED REPOSITORY LEVELS

With an understanding of the objects to be tracked and the role they play in modeling, the model management team should begin to determine the levels of repositories they need to maintain. Two areas need to be considered in this analysis. First, what levels of integration does the organization need to achieve by object type? Second, what levels of integration are feasible?

Ideally, all objects would be maintained at a corporate level. However, as discussed in Chapter 7, this is often not practical. Not all objects can be ensured to be unique across all projects in the corporation. The model managers should identify those that require true corporate-wide uniqueness, those that can be unique across all applications in a business area, those that can be unique across all projects in an application, and those that are project-specific. For data objects, uniqueness by subject area may also be a consideration, since data objects could be grouped logically and maintained at a level lower than corporate-wide while still providing more integration than a process-oriented grouping, such as business area or application.

The matrix in Figure 8.2 can be used to analyze actual project model integration requirements. Each of the major object types and linkage types should be analyzed to see if it needs to be unique across projects, across all projects in an application, across all applications in a business area, or across all business areas. Data

	Cross Project	Cross Application	Cross Business Area	Cross Subject Area
Conceptual Data Objects				
Conceptual Process Objects				
Logical Data Objects				
Logical Process Objects				
Physical Data Objects				
Physical Process Objects				
Conceptual Data-Process Link				
Logical Data-Process Link				
Physical Data-Process Link				
Conceptual-Logical Data Link				
Conceptual-Logical Process Link				
Logical-Physical Data Link				
Logical-Physical Process Link				

Figure 8.2.   Association Matrix Diagrammer: object integration requirements.

objects may also be analyzed across all subject areas. This table could be expanded to illustrate actual objects and linkages that are to be contained at each level. Optionally, corporate information models could be developed for each level.

Any object or linkage type that needs to be unique across all business areas or subject areas requires corporate-level control. Object or linkage types that require, at most, cross-application control are candidates for business-area or subject-area repositories. Cross-project control objects show the need for application-level repositories.

If corporate repositories are identified, it is important to identify if multiples are needed. For example, both modules and logical data objects may need to be tracked at a corporate level. Since these two objects have no relationship, it may be feasible to maintain them in separate corporate-level repositories. Separate repositories may be desirable if different individuals are responsible for maintenance of these two objects or if repository size is limited.

In some cases, separate corporate repositories may be required. If the organization maintains a set of planning models that depict the future business and its information requirements, some of the same objects as those in the current corporate models may be used. Unless naming standards distinguish between a current and future object, such as the current version of the EMPLOYEE entity and the future version of the EMPLOYEE entity, the current and future models may need to be separated.

STEP 3: EVALUATE ORGANIZATIONAL OBJECTIVES

Is the organization moving toward an integrated database philosophy?

If the organization is striving for integrated databases, the data model components of the information model will be critical. This also implies that it is important to track data usage across projects. A corporate-wide repository of data information is necessary. A business area or project level may be sufficient for nondata objects, but a mechanism must be in place to track where the integrated objects are used and when they are being revised. Nonintegrated data groups are not necessarily required at the corporate level.

If integrated data is not an issue, business-area or project-based repositories may provide a sufficient level of control. However, once projects begin to use data objects independently and these objects are stored in multiple repositories without control, the implementation of control mechanisms in the future to achieve an integrated data environment will be difficult. An alternative for organizations that are not yet prepared to implement unique data across applications but would like that flexibility in the future is to develop a set of naming standards for data objects that would assist in identifying duplicate information.

Is the organization moving toward reusable modules of program code?

Reusable subroutines have been a source of programmer efficiency for years. Implementing the same concept at the specification level has the potential to achieve the same type of efficiencies. However, effective coordination of these modules will require control similar to that used in subroutine source code. A corporate-wide repository housing common modules would be required if the modules are shared by all applications. Business Area common module repositories may be sufficient if modules will not be shared across applications supporting different business areas. An organization may elect to have both corporate and business-area common module repositories. These may be combined with other objects, such as integrated data objects in the corporate repository.

Is the organization implementing code generation?

In a code generation environment, control of the specifications becomes much more critical. They are no longer documentation but are actually the source for the object code. Therefore, strict control will be required over specification objects. In addition, the data objects referenced by the specifications will also require tight control since a change to a physical data object may affect multiple specifications, thereby changing a great deal of object code. The organization must carefully develop standards and procedures to ensure this high degree of control.

Will specifications, not source code, be maintained?

Some organizations may decide that tight control over specifications is not feasible in their environment. Others may be using tools that make the rapid maintenance of specifications difficult in production troubleshooting situations. These environments may to use specifications initially elect to generate code but then maintain the resulting source code. In these organizations, the control over specifications is no longer critical and the burden of model management is greatly reduced. However, the benefits derived from maintaining high-level specifications instead of detailed code will be lost.

Has a conceptual data and/or process model been created for the organization or will one be created in the future?

The task of developing conceptual models, especially for the entire organization, can be very time-consuming. Often firms wish to be able to store these models for future use. A conceptual model repository would therefore be required.

This repository may be one of the existing repositories. However, it is important to ensure uniqueness of conceptual objects across all objects that might be in the repository. For example, if entities were used to capture data groups in the conceptual model and were also used in logical data modeling, the data group EMPLOYEE may conflict with the entity EMPLOYEE. Therefore, careful naming standards and object usage need to be identified to effectively combine the conceptual repository with any other repository.

If so, does the organization need to maintain any portion of the model at least annually for decision-making purposes?

Static models that do not require maintenance are relatively easy to manage. Integrity is ensured at the time of development and potential conflicts with existing repositories are easily identified so that the model resides in the correct location. However, if the model is to be maintained, standards and procedures must be established to ensure that integrity is maintained and that conflicts with other models in the same repository are minimized.

If the conceptual models are to be used as the starting point for subsequent development projects, maintenance to the model may potentially be a more important consideration. To implement changes in the model to all projects currently using the model, a means of tracking which project is using which portion of the conceptual model is vital. In this environment, project teams must be willing to accept any rework that arises from changes to the conceptual model. In many organizations, this may not be realistic except in projects that are still in the initial stages of development. An alternative is to allow conceptual model changes to affect all *new* projects, but not projects that are already underway unless a major change is detected that could have a dramatic impact on the way the system is used by the organization in the future.

STEP 4: EVALUATE CASE TOOL SUPPORT OF MODEL MANAGEMENT

How many CASE tools are in use today?

Model management in organizations using a single integrated CASE tool set will be relatively straightforward. For the majority of organizations, multiple CASE tools will be in use. Model management will have responsibility for integrating models across tools as required, thereby requiring a larger model management staff familiar with all aspects of the various tools.

How many CASE tools are planned for future implementation?

Although a limited number of CASE tools may be implemented today, organizations should recognize the long-term potential for a number of specialized CASE tools. If expansion of the CASE tool portfolio is planned for the near future, the model manager should be involved in the tool evaluation decisions to ensure that any new tools work within existing model management directions. Once the tool is selected, the model manager must determine how to control any new models that are now available. This also implies additional responsibility for the model management staff.

What platforms do these tools utilize?

If all tools utilize the same platform, such as an OS/2 based workstation with a database manager model storage platform, identifying how to manage models across tools is limited in scope. However, model managers seeking to control models that can be developed and maintained on multiple platforms have a complex task. For example, logical models may be developed on a workstation. Database design may occur in a tool on a mainframe. Code generation may occur on a network. Another project may target a different environment, designing databases and program specifications on a midrange platform. The model manager must identify whether these models need to be merged into a single location and, if so, how they will be maintained.

From a project model development perspective, are single or multiple repositories used?

If a single repository is used by all members of a project team, the model management activities focus on coordinating duplicate maintenance of shared objects. However, a model manager supporting multiple-project repositories must constantly be concerned with merging shared objects and resolving model conflicts. This greatly increases the amount of time required to ensure project model accuracy.

How much automation does the CASE tool provide for merging models?

Managing duplicate objects across projects and tools is greatly facilitated by automated merging facilities. At a project level, automated merging makes sharing of models among developers using workstations easier. If the facilities also assist in migrating models from one tool to another, the model manager's tasks are also reduced. At a corporate level, any facility that combines models from multiple projects will provide labor savings.

Is there a single repository location available at the corporate level?

If a single facility is available with the capability to track all objects and linkages of interest to the organization, the corporate model manager can focus on the issues of model merging and integrity. However, if multiple storage locations are used, the model manager must ensure the consistency of the models across the repositories. This additional task can prove very time-consuming unless automated integration facilities are available.

For organizations using the KnowledgeWare tool, a corporate encyclopedia could be developed at the PC or mainframe level. However, if multiple CASE tools are used and objects within the KnowledgeWare tool do not correspond directly to objects in the other CASE tool, it may be difficult to utilize KnowledgeWare's encyclopedia as a single repository for all corporate models.

If not, should one be purchased or developed?

There is an increasing number of vendors who are marketing repositories on common platforms. However, these repositories may not match the organization's information model. In these cases, the repository tool may include some user-defined objects that can be used to expand the available objects. It may also be possible to develop files that include extensions to the tool.

If a suitable tool cannot be found or customized, the organization has the option of developing its own corporate repository. If the corporate information model is relatively simple and the CASE tools in use provide a relatively simple mechanism for extracting information from the tool, this may be a viable option for the organization. This approach has the advantage of being capable of automating the checking of many standards that are in use in the organization and may therefore provide the best long-term solution to model management. However, the developers will need to develop their own merging algorithms, which can prove to be a time-consuming task. In addition, as new CASE tools are acquired or as CASE tools support new features, the repository must be modified.

Does the CASE tool have any limitations on model or repository size?

This is an important question that is often overlooked by CASE tool purchasers. Features and functionality tend to overwhelm a new user, and tool constraints are downplayed by the vendor. If the tool does have a maximum model or repository size, a single corporate repository is probably impossible. If a corporate level is needed, a small, critical subset of the total object set needs to be identified as the corporate level. Business Area or Application repositories will be required for all other objects.

In some tools this limitation may be so restrictive that an entire project model may not fit into a single repository. In this case, the organization needs to identify which project model objects are required in the long run. Perhaps specifications, screen layouts, and database definitions are required for maintenance purposes, but logical models may not be maintained. If the logical models are to be maintained, perhaps a separate logical model repository can be established. Tradeoffs will exist in any compromise situation. If logical models are stored separately, the linkage between the physical and logical cannot be easily tracked.

Although limitations on encyclopedia size were inherent in KnowledgeWare's DOS software, the OS/2- and mainframe-based tools do not have the same size limitations. Although processing time may be greater for larger size encyclopedias, the tools can now handle extremely large encyclopedias, such as those required at a corporate level.

Is there a data dictionary in place that already handles some of the model management activities for data objects?

The implementation of a data dictionary addresses many of the same issues involved in repository implementation. The organization has been sold on the importance of standards and procedures to maintain the integrity of the data dictionary. Now the discipline needs to be expanded to include all objects. If the data dictionary is successful, the organization has likely already understood the importance of a data dictionary support staff, which is similar to the model management staff. The net result is easier model management implementation with a potentially smaller staff size.

If so, do you plan to continue use of the data dictionary in the future?

Although the existence of a data dictionary can assist the implementation of model management, organizations that elect to maintain both a centralized repository and a separate data dictionary will face a unique set of problems. While ensuring integrity of the models in the repositories is complex, ensuring that the repositories are in synch with the data dictionary is a tremendous undertaking.

Careful procedures are needed to ensure that all updates to one are also made to the other. Either the data dictionary or the repository needs to be established as the source of the data model. The other will always be a copy. In addition to procedures, responsibilities need to be carefully defined if Data Administration has control over the data dictionary and model management controls the repositories. This is a situation of redundant data and should be managed as carefully as any redundant data implemented in production systems.

Are there any other tools that may contain model information?

If the organization's information model includes physical data and process objects, other tools that support source and database management should be considered as potential sources of model information. These tools contain information that could be used to validate the integrity of the models contained in the corporate repositories and are therefore important from the model management perspective. Objects could be added to the information model to track these objects and the relationship they have to the models maintained in the CASE tools. They should also be considered when developing procedures for model maintenance since facilities could be purchased or developed that automate the integrity checking of models based on the content of these tools.

Other sources of model integrity checking should also be evaluated. Published corporate plans may be used to validate future or conceptual models. Project management packages that may include information such as a detailed list of all programs to be developed by a project. Any manual or automated integration points are worthy of documentation.

STEP 5: EVALUATE CASE TOOL SUPPORT FOR THE INFORMATION MODEL

How is each object supported by a CASE tool?

If the information models were derived from models produced by CASE tools, it should be relatively easy to identify how existing

CASE tools support the objects. However, if some objects are not currently in use, it may be more difficult to identify CASE tool support. Model managers should identify unsupported objects as well as duplicate objects.

Suppose the organization considers a project plan stored in a project management tool as a project model. Although the project and resources can be represented within the KnowledgeWare Planning Workstation, all the time management and reporting features do not map to a KnowledgeWare object. A decision must be made about how this information will be maintained long-term and if the Project Object will be maintained redundantly in KnowledgeWare as a link between the project management model and the actual project development models.

What objects are duplicated across tools?

The more that objects are duplicated across tools, the more difficult model management becomes. If data structures are developed in an Upper CASE tool, then used by a prototyper in a Lower CASE tool and by a database optimizer tool, the same information is duplicated in three places. The model manager must determine which tool is the primary source where maintenance will occur and how changes will be merged into the other tools.

Organizations implementing KnowledgeWare's Design Workstation for development, and another Database Administration tool to fully document physical database design, must identify the other CASE tool as the primary source of physical data information. This information should then be merged to KnowledgeWare through an automated facility or manual maintenance so that it is available for the developers to use in Screen and Report layouts and specifications.

Does it make sense to link these duplicate objects?

Once a duplicate maintenance situation such as the one outlined above is identified, the model manager should evaluate the benefit gained by keeping the same model in multiple places. A critical issue is whether the model is needed for linkages in all locations. For example, the physical database design may be linked to the logical data model in the Upper CASE tool. The Lower CASE tool may link the database components to the appropriate Screens and Reports. If both the logical model and the screen and report layouts are to be maintained through the CASE tools, duplication of the database design may be required. However, the version that resides in the database optimization tool may only be required when database analysis is underway. This model may be loaded into the optimizer tool as required, instead of being continuously maintained there.

What objects are not supported by existing CASE tools?

Although it may appear that objects are not supported, it may in fact be that the organization has not yet implemented an available portion of the CASE tool. The vendor may be able to help the organization identify such objects. If the object is not supported, the organization may need to consider the purchase of additional CASE tools or the expansion of existing tools if allowed by the vendor.

Should the information model be modified to work with the existing set of CASE tools?

As a last option, the organization may need to readdress its information model to work within the constraints of implemented CASE tools. Since the model was developed to meet the needs of the organization, the organizational goals and priorities should be evaluated prior to making any changes to the information model.

Using the project management model example mentioned earlier, the organization may determine that this model is not a part of the organization's information model. Alternatively, the organization may decide that only the Project object itself is a part of the information model and will be maintained with all other model objects through the KnowledgeWare tool.

STEP 6: EVALUATE CASE TOOL SUPPORT FOR THE ACTIVITY MODEL

Which tools support each model management activity?

Some model management tasks will be manual, but a majority should have some CASE tool support. The model manager should identify the extent of the support and determine if additional facilities are needed. These may include the development of reports that compare models, a project tracking system, and a model merging tool.

How much automation does the CASE tool provide for merging models?

Managing duplicate objects across projects and tools is greatly facilitated by automated merging facilities. At a project level, automated merging makes sharing of models among developers using workstations easier. If the facilities also assist in migrating models from one tool to another, the model manager's tasks are also reduced. At a corporate level, any facility that combines models from multiple projects will provide labor savings.

What other facilities are automatically supported?

Possible facilities include standards checking and duplicate identification. These facilities should be compared to the organization's requirements. A tool may seem to provide adequate facilities, but it may use a set of standards or a technique of identifying duplicates that is inconsistent with the organization's direction.

Should the activity model be modified to work with the existing set of CASE tools?

The model management team may decide that too many manual procedures are required with existing CASE tools. As with information model changes, this should be considered only after all other alternatives have been evaluated.

PRACTICAL EXAMPLE #1: SINGLE-TOOL ENVIRONMENT

In this first example, a possible model management strategy for an organization with a single CASE tool will be explained. The organization has decided to maintain logical and physical data models, process models, and linkage models. The specific objects for each of the models have been identified and each object was found to have only one use. Data models and physical process models were found to be unique across all applications in all business areas due to existing naming standards. Logical process models and logical linkage models, such as dataflow diagrams, were only unique at the business-area level. Therefore, a two-tier approach to corporate repositories was selected. A business area would represent a group of applications development teams which were already aligned with the major areas of the business.

An integrated database environment is a top priority for the business which is striving to improve communications throughout the organization. This is consistent with the selection of a single, corporate-wide data repository. Code generation is not yet a reality for the organization, but it would like to move in that direction in the future. Therefore, the physical process and linkage models will be maintained in the same corporate-wide repository.

The organization currently uses a single, integrated CASE tool. Using this tool, the applications development teams target both IBM and DEC environments. The CASE tool provides automated model merging based on name matching. No data dictionary is in place. At this time, the number of models the firm has developed is relatively small, so the corporate repository and business area repositories will reside on a file server, controlled by a model management team. All models, regardless of their targeted environment, will be included in this environment. The organization understands that full implementation of code generation on both platforms may require a reassessment of the repository storage location.

The tool requires that each analyst have his or her own project repository. Therefore, it is expected that a member of the model management team will work closely with project teams to ensure effective management of shared objects. This will also allow the model managers to be aware of changes to existing models.

The CASE tool supports the relationships illustrated in the corporate information model. However, it does not require definitions for all objects and does not include name-standard conformance checking. The model management team will investigate outside vendor software that can provide this additional level of integrity checking in a more automated fashion. The vendor's software provides a check-in/check-out feature that tracks usage of an object by multiple individuals. Procedures will be carefully designed to require all project teams to request a version of the corporate models for their work.

PRACTICAL EXAMPLE #2: MULTIPLE-TOOL ENVIRONMENT

This organization uses two CASE tools, an Upper CASE and a Lower CASE tool. Conceptual and logical data and process models are developed in the Upper CASE tool. Screens, Reports, PseudoCode, and Physical data definitions are maintained in the Lower CASE tool. All models are unique at the business-area level. Only limited common subroutines are used across all applications. Interface files transfer data between the different applications. The organization is implementing code generation with no source code maintenance. Therefore, business-area repositories will be established with strict control over access to production versions of physical models.

Each tool provides automated merging of models. An interface is available to take logical data models from the Upper CASE tool to the Lower CASE tool. The organization views logical data models as a starting point for physical design but does not emphasize the use of logical data models once the physical model has been developed. Logical process and linkage models are seen as analysis tools but are not usually maintained once the physical system design has begun. Therefore, only physical data, process, and linkage models will be maintained at a corporate level. Project-level repositories containing logical models will be kept on backup diskettes for use in later projects if applicable. A manual list of the available logical models will be maintained. Therefore, from a corporate model maintenance perspective, the model management staff is concerned only with the validity of the models stored in the Lower CASE tool. The staff will still assist the project teams in project model management for the Upper CASE tool, since it requires that multiple project repositories be implemented.

PRACTICAL EXAMPLE #3: IN-HOUSE DEVELOPED REPOSITORY

The third organization recently purchased a new company, its second major acquisition in the past three years. It is the direction of the organization to combine the systems used by these organizations into a single, integrated set of applications that meet the unique needs of the different groups. Each of the three Information Systems groups uses its own set of CASE tools. The organization is attempting to select a single set for long-range development, but a variety of tools will likely be in use for some time in the future.

Existing business models were identified as a top-priority model management issue, since they contain vital information about how the different groups function and can hopefully be used as a starting point for the new, consolidated applications. Similar approaches are used for data and process models in each tool. Very different approaches to logical linkage objects have been taken. The physical models appear to be so different that integration into a single corporate information model is unrealistic. The initial target of model management will be the development of an information model that will support logical models. A special linkage model will be developed that includes all techniques of linkage. Different components will be populated by different CASE tools. An in-house repository will be developed and a team will be established to develop and maintain the repository and the merging routines. Division-level repositories will be used initially, one per company. Model managers will manage physical models within the confines of the CASE tool used to develop the model.

A model management database will also be developed in-house to track the existence of models and to make the models available for use by development teams. The model management staff will review standards in place by the various groups and will attempt to develop a single, long-term standard that will be implemented gradually over time. Some portions of the standards may be applied retroactively to existing models if resources are available to make the transition. However, the emphasis will be placed on ensuring consistency and validity of new models developed under the new CASE direction.

The Model Management Staff

A TYPICAL MODEL MANAGER'S DAY

7:15 A.M.   The model manager arrives at the office to merge new versions of commonly used subroutines to all analyst repositories. The manager would have finished before the analysts arrived for the day if technical difficulties had not been encountered with one PC.

9:30 A.M.   Technical problems with the final PC have been resolved and the analyst, who blamed the model manager for the delay, has been calmed. One of the other analysts calls, frantically claiming that the model manager has deleted all his specifications.

10:15 A.M.   After discovering that the analyst was looking in the wrong repository, the model manager begins to work on her next task for the day, moving completed project models to the corporate repository.

11:00 A.M.   Several discrepancies were found between the existing corporate models and the project models. The model manager goes in search of the project leader.

11:30 A.M.   The project leader is on vacation, but two analysts have said that they don't think the model manager has the correct version of the project models. They will search for the correct set when they get a chance.

11:45 A.M.   The model manager prepares to merge a new project data model to analyst models during lunch. All analysts on the project team are called to arrange times for the merge. One analyst plans to work through lunch, so special arrangements are made to complete his merge after work.

1:15 P.M.   One analyst had incorrectly used data objects on his screen layouts. The model manager assists the analyst in modifying all seven of his screen definitions using data objects correctly. He is behind in his work, so his data model merge will also have to be completed after work.

1:45 P.M.   The model manager grabs a bite to eat at her desk while reviewing an update to the corporate standards manual that explains standards for linking specifications and data objects.

2:00 P.M.   A flashy demonstration is presented by a competitor of the organization's Upper CASE tool vendor. The competitor explains how easy it would be to migrate to his product or even use the two in combination. The model manager tries to maintain her composure, and asks targeted questions about true model compatibility.

3:15 P.M.   The analysts from the completed project return with the "correct" version of their models. Unfortunately, their backups include only data models that were last updated three months ago.

3:40 P.M.   The model manager is stopped in the hall by the CIO, who is praising the competitor's CASE tool. She sets up a meeting for next week to allow the model manager to explain why she is so concerned.

4:00 P.M.   The model manager meets with a new project team that will be using models for the first time. She helps them develop an education plan and agrees on the level of assistance the team will require. A team member is selected to assist the model manager in the development of a project information model.

5:00 P.M. The model manager completes the final two data model merges.

5:45 P.M. The model manager leaves for home with her portable PC to complete time-consuming model merges overnight.

Although this eleven-hour day may seem unrealistic, it is common for many members of model management teams. Daily, the model manager must deal with both corporate and project model management issues. As the example illustrates, these tasks move beyond the actual management of the models and include participation in application development strategy decisions such as the selection of new CASE tools, and in the continuing definition of model standards and procedures.

RESPONSIBILITIES AT THE PROJECT LEVEL

The model manager supporting a project is responsible for ensuring that all team members have access to the objects and linkages they need as they are required. In addition to supporting the team itself, the project model manager must also ensure that the project models conform to corporate standards and can be merged with other existing models.

To support these two aspects of project model management, it is important that the project model manager begins by assisting the team in the development of a project information model. This involves a review of the project goals and the methodology to be used. The appropriate deliverables can then be identified. The model manager uses this information to develop the project information model, clearly documenting the types of models to be developed and the requirements of the model objects. The information model may be developed at the start of each phase or may be developed for all phases at project startup.

Once the information model is in place, the project model manager needs to analyze the need for project-specific standards. One or more special repositories may be required. Standard project prefixes may be needed for module names. In some cases, corporate-wide standards may not work for the project or may need to be expanded. The project model manager should coordinate any required corporate changes before implementing them at a project level.

On a daily basis, the project model manager is responsible for maintaining common models across analysts. Although the actual changes may be made by a project team member, the project model manager will ensure that all other team members who may be affected by the change are consulted and that the most recent version is available to all team members. If multiple-project repositories are used, the project model manager is responsible for merging models across repositories. In the example at the beginning of this chapter, the model manager merged commonly used routines for one project and data models for another. These merges had to be coordinated to minimize the impact on the team's development efforts.

The project model manager is responsible for ensuring that project and corporate-wide model standards are met. Shared models can be inspected at the time they are distributed to individual analysts. The model manager should also periodically inspect nonshared models to ensure that they conform to standards. In the example above, the model manager took the opportunity to review object use as she merged a commonly used data model to individual analyst workstations. Once an error was found, the model manager then had to spend time explaining the error and assisting the analyst in quickly correcting the problem.

Any potential changes to existing corporate-level models should be identified by the project model manager and the project team as soon as possible so changes can be discussed with other groups that may be affected. For example, a change to a highly integrated piece of the corporate data model may affect several current and completed projects. It may not be feasible for all affected areas to react in the time frame assumed by the team initiating the change.

At project completion or phase completion, the model manager is responsible for assisting with the merging of the project models with the corporate models. On a project level, this involves preparing the project models for the merge. Often this requires the merging of multiple project models to one single project model. Difficulties at this stage range from problems finding the correct version of the model, as experienced by the model manager at the beginning of the chapter, to violations of standards found after project completion.

RESPONSIBILITIES AT THE CORPORATE LEVEL

Corporate model management involves many of the same responsibilities as project model management but on a much broader scale. Instead of dealing with the models of a single project team, the corporate model manager must deal with all models developed by all project teams. In addition, the corporate model manager must make corporate-level models easily available for inquiry and maintenance purposes to individuals across Information Systems and the business community.

The development of the corporate information model is the first responsibility for corporate model managers. This model will identify which models will be kept at which corporate level. It becomes the blueprint for how the corporate model manager will perform daily activities. It also serves as the foundation for project information models.

With this model in place, the corporate model manager needs to develop the standards and procedures that support this model. Careful attention should be given to how these standards integrate with existing standards and should be as close as possible to minimize confusion. Procedures should work smoothly with any existing procedures, most importantly with the systems development methodology. Standards and procedures should address both model development and maintenance across all projects.

When a project begins, the corporate model manager is responsible for helping the team create its initial project models from existing models. Since the team is likely to be unfamiliar with the available corporate models, the corporate model manager must have a strong knowledge of existing models and how they may be of use to the project team.

With a model potentially being changed simultaneously by multiple projects, the corporate model manager must track model usage across projects. The manager must also retain sufficiently close contact with each team to identify potential changes to shared objects and linkages and then coordinate changes across the projects. A strong change control process combined with a good working relationship with project model managers can greatly facilitate this activity.

Once a project or a project phase is complete, the corporate model manager must evaluate the resulting models. First the manager must ensure that all corporate model requirements are met. If the model includes additional components that are not required at a corporate level, the corporate model manager must work with the team to evaluate the feasibility of storing those additional components at a corporate level. Any changes to other models must then be evaluated with the assistance of the project team. Hopefully, all these changes were approved prior to project model completion. The resulting models are then merged into the appropriate corporate models and any required changes to other models are completed.

The model manager must constantly reevaluate the model management strategy. New corporate levels may be required. Old assumptions regarding required business areas may no longer apply. Standards may not work consistently with new CASE tools. Changes to procedures may be required as a result of a change to the corporate methodology. A new release of the CASE tool vendor's information model may result in a change to the organization's information model. The corporate model manager must be involved in the appropriate decision-making activities so that these types of changes can be analyzed and implemented as required.

MODEL MANAGEMENT SKILLS

To effectively serve the organization in a model management role, an individual needs to possess a wide variety of Information Systems and business skills. One of the most important is an understanding of the models that are produced. This includes an in-depth knowledge of the organization's information model. The manager must know the objects and linkages that are required and those that are optional and must be able to analyze the impact to the overall model of specific changes. For example, if a change is made to a logical data model object, the model manager must be able to assess the corresponding impact to the dataflow diagrams, physical database design, specifications, and screen and report layouts.

It is helpful if model managers have prior experience in data dictionary maintenance. Many of the object and linkage management skills of model management are basically an extension of the data model management skills developed by Data Administration groups in the past. In addition to understanding the information model, the model manager, like the data dictionary manager, must also be able to understand the technical and conceptual aspects of model merging, object and linkage maintenance, and the management of multiple versions.

Often model managers become the experts in modeling techniques. They need to understand the analysis and design activities performed within the organization and how models support those activities. A detailed knowledge of the organization's methodology and the rationale behind the supporting modeling approaches can be critical in helping the model manager assist a team in understanding why they need to develop a model according to model management standards and procedures.

As in many CASE implementation roles, the model manager serves as a salesperson for the use of CASE in the organization. The individual must therefore be enthusiastic about the new technologies and techniques being implemented and must be capable of conveying the enthusiasm to others in the organization. However, the model manager must not be so enamored of the technology that he or she overlooks the importance of the models themselves. Unlike the research group that may select the CASE tools and make them work technically, the model manager is more concerned with the underlying information model of the tool and how that works with the corporate information model.

For corporate model management, it is important that the individual understands the existing models that are in place, at least at a conceptual level. This will help the manager better merge models and create initial project models in an environment striving for integration and reusability. Information Systems development teams can be helpful in providing details of how systems interact, but the model manager must be in a position to involve the appropriate groups when decisions need to be made about objects and linkages.

In addition to understanding the systems, it is also helpful if the model manager understands the business itself. If logical models are maintained at the corporate level, the model manager must be in a position to evaluate changes to business-oriented as well as to systems-oriented models. A detailed understanding of all aspects of the business is not required, but knowledge of major functions and data of the business, and how different areas of the business interact, assists the model manager in identifying the required levels of corporate models and analyzing changes to models at those levels.

Due to the very detailed aspects of model management functions, an individual who enjoys detailed problem solving is better suited to daily model management activities than a conceptual thinker. Someone who is theoretical may be helpful in developing the initial information model and the high-level standards and procedures, but will likely become bored performing the day-to-day maintenance activities.

The model manager should also be someone who enjoys working with others tactfully. The model manager is often put in the position of a mediator between a group with a proposed change and the groups that will be affected by the change. As illustrated in the example at the beginning of the chapter, the model manager often becomes the scapegoat for problems, including technical PC problems that are unrelated to model management. Even the most experienced model manager will occasionally make an error in merging that will cause a delay in development activities. Like a star programmer who has temporarily caused downtime in a major application, the model manager must face criticism from some of the business's harshest critics, the Information Systems professionals.

SAMPLE MODEL MANAGEMENT POSITIONS

Figures 9.1 and 9.2 are possible job descriptions for corporate model management functions. The first is a corporate model administrator. This job is responsible for the high-level activities of corporate model management, such as developing the information model, establishing higher-level standards and procedures, and resolving conflicts between teams. The corporate model manager

---

Job Title: Corporate Model Administrator

Responsibilities:

1. Coordinate the definition of model management standards and procedures.
2. Lead the implementation of model management standards and procedures.
3. Provide project teams with access to corporate-level models and support their development of project-level models.
4. Provide the business with access to corporate-level models as required.
5. Train the Information Systems staff on model management concepts, standards, and procedures.
6. Supervise the model management staff, including the model management analysts and project model managers.

Experience:

4–6 years of system analysis experience including the development and use of models.

1–2 years of managerial experience.

1–2 years of project management experience.

1–2 years of project management experience.

Data and/or Process Administration experience preferred.

Figure 9.1.   Job Description : Corporate Model Administrator.

in this scenario would also be responsible for managing the model management staff.

The corporate model management analyst deals more with the daily activities of model management. The analyst coordinates the detailed changes across multiple projects, ensures that standards and procedures are followed, and serves as consultant to project model managers. An analyst would be responsible for the actual merging of models.

These two positions could be implemented in a variety of ways. The organization could have a model administrator and multiple model analysts. The analysts could have responsibility for a set of

---

Job Title: Corporate Model Management Analyst

Reports to: Corporate Model Administrator

Responsibilities:
1. Participate in the definition of model management standards and procedures.
2. Support the implementation of model management standards by ensuring model conformance to standards and model integrity.
3. Support the implementation of model management procedures by merging project-level models to the appropriate corporate-level models when required, and providing both project teams and the business with access to models upon request.
4. Support all project model development activities to ensure conformance to standards and procedures. Either serve as the project model manager or assist the project model manager.
5. Assist in the training of the Information Systems staff on model management concepts, standards, and procedures.

Experience:
2–3 years of system analysis experience including the development and use of models.
Data and/or Process Administration experience preferred.

Figure 9.2.   Job Description : Model Management Analyst.

business areas or applications, such as a Finance Model Analyst, a Marketing Model Analyst, and a Manufacturing Model Analyst (Figure 9.3), or may have responsibility for a set of model types, such as a Data Model Analyst and a Process Model Analyst (Figure 9.4) or a Logical Model Analyst and a Physical Model Analyst (Figure 9.5). The corporate model management analysts may serve as the project model managers or may supervise their activities. If model analysts are not feasible in the initial startup of model management, the corporate model administrator can directly or indirectly supervise project model managers who are members of the project team (Figure 9.6).

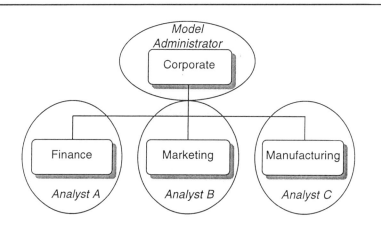

Figure 9.3.   Responsibility by Application.

The use of clerical personnel or interns can prove helpful in providing additional support to the model management staff. While the planning and control of model merging require the guidance of a skilled model manager, the actual execution of the merge can be performed by a less technical individual. If manual

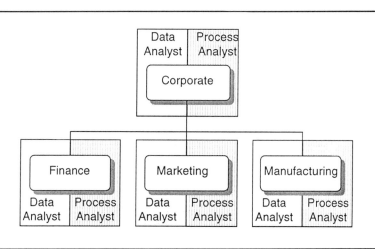

Figure 9.4.   Data and Process Model Management.

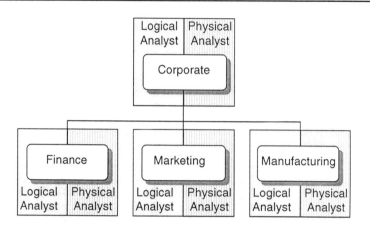

Figure 9.5. Logical and Physical Model Management.

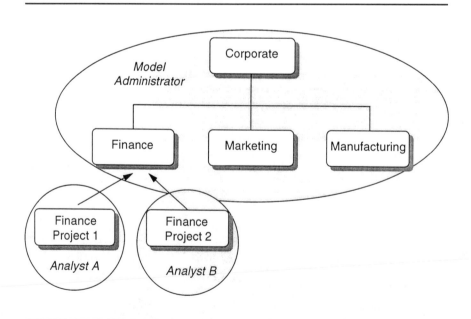

Figure 9.6. Corporate Model Management with Project Model Managers.

model maintenance is required, this can also be performed by a support person. Manual checking for conformance to clearly specified standards can also be performed by someone other than the model manager. College interns can be especially helpful in these types of roles since they are usually familiar with mouse-driven software, commonly used as the foundation for workstation-based CASE tools, and therefore have a relatively small learning curve if their actions are carefully directed.

POSITIONING MODEL MANAGEMENT WITHIN THE ORGANIZATION

The position of model management within the organization's reporting structure can be critical to its success. Due to its similarity to source management, an option may be to position the team as an extension of source management or as a separate team within the same reporting structure. The drawback to this approach is the tendency of organizations to consider source management as a production control or technical center area. Although model management, especially within a code generation environment, does have some production control aspects, it is actually better defined as a development and end-user support group.

Model management is probably better aligned with support groups such as Database Administration. It provides many of the same types of control and support services, but instead of providing data it provides models to help design system components, including data. This positioning is consistent with model management's strong support of the applications development and maintenance efforts.

If the business is heavily involved in model development and maintenance, model management could also be viewed as an extension of the end-user computing function. However, this positioning may tend to isolate the model manager from the application developer, who is the primary client of model management in most environments.

It is important to place model management in a position of authority. The model manager must be able to decline changes requested by the business and by the Information Systems group. If model management is positioned at the same level as a development analyst, this type of authority may not be recognized. Even positioning the team at the level of project managers may not be sufficient to provide the perceived authority level that will be critical in the initial startup phases. The optimal approach may be to place the model management team at the same level as senior management within the Information Systems organization. This provides the necessary authority level in the eyes of both the business and the Information Systems group.

MANAGEMENT'S RESPONSIBILITIES

To allow model management to proceed effectively in the organization, management in both Information Systems and the business community have responsibilities. The most important is to actively support the development of models as a part of the systems analysis and development process. In some organizations, management places an emphasis on final system implementation. An equal emphasis must be placed on the analysis and design activities and the associated deliverables. These modeling activities must be viewed as vital contributors to the end result, an efficient implemented system that meets the requirements of the business.

Once management has committed itself to the development of the models, it must then expand its support to include the model management activities. From a management perspective, this involves providing sufficient resources to perform these activities. Resources include time during project development to manage project-level models, time to coordinate model use across projects, and time to support model maintenance which results from application maintenance.

One of the most critical resources is the model management staff itself. If feasible, dedicated individuals should be assigned to the model management team. These individuals should be given the appropriate training to ensure their success.

Effective model management may also require the purchase of additional software and hardware to support the management of large, corporate-level models. Once these resources are acquired, management must dedicate sufficient resources to maintain the hardware and software. Although the models themselves may not be seen as critical as a production application, they do represent the foundation for that application and therefore are of equal, long-term importance to the organization. If the organization decides to develop some model management tools itself, management also needs to dedicate the resources to support the development and maintenance activities.

In addition to supporting the physical resources, management also needs to voice its support of the model management activities. This includes supporting the development of an information model at the corporate and project levels to clearly document the types of deliverables that will be managed. Strong support of the standards and procedures required for model management are also necessary. Team members must know that shortcuts to achieve on-time project implementation should not be used in these areas.

The Special Role of Middle Management

The support of middle Information Systems management is vital to the success of model management activities. These managers, who are directly responsible for project development teams, are the individuals who are generally held accountable for timely project implementation within a strict budget. The development of models can potentially affect these goals dramatically. If new CASE tools are required, the project budget can expand. If the developers are unfamiliar with the tool or modeling, the total project time may be increased. If modeling requires direct involvement with the business and the business's time is limited, project completion may also be delayed.

Middle management should also understand that the resulting models can, in the long run, improve project team performance. By providing better documentation, maintenance to the resulting system is expedited. The quality improvements in terms of system design and user requirements should also result in a decrease in required maintenance and enhancement time. Future projects can reuse the models developed by the project team, decreasing their overall development time.

Senior management can assist in encouraging middle management to support modeling efforts by emphasizing the longer-term benefits. In addition to implementation dates and budgets, middle managers could also be measured by more quality-oriented factors, such as overall business satisfaction with a system and the maintenance cost of the system. Both senior management and the business should also be aware of the short-term costs of modeling and CASE tool introduction and should set their project date and budget expectations accordingly.

10

Alternatives for Model Management Implementation

EVALUATION OF THE EXISTING INFORMATION SYSTEMS STRUCTURE

The ideal model management implementation scenario may be a single, centralized model management team that provides all model management functions across all projects in the organization. However, there are several teams that may be in existence today that may already be performing limited model management functions. These groups may either provide valuable assistance to the model management function or may become stumbling blocks if they are not effectively coordinated with the model management team.

Data Administration

An increasing number of organizations are implementing Data Administration groups to help them better manage their data resources. Traditional Data Administration functions include strategic data planning, project data analysis support, and logical data modeling. They are typically the owners of the corporate data dictionary, which tracks the definition of logical and physical data structures.

Data Administration is separated from the Database Administration group by a difference in emphasis. The Database Administration team focuses on the efficient implementation of user requirements. The team's expertise lies in technical knowledge of one or more database platforms. Data Administration focuses more on defining business requirements for data and tracking information across projects and platforms.

Organizations may position their Data Administration function as a support group or as an active data modeling team. If the applications development teams are knowledgeable in data modeling techniques, the Data Administration group may provide support as needed and may coordinate data model development across projects. In environments where applications teams are less familiar with data analysis concepts such as normalization, the organization may decide to implement a relatively large Data Administration team. In this environment, members of the Data Administration group may be assigned responsibility for project data model development. In organizations striving to develop a set of subject databases, the Data Administration team may be assigned responsibility for defining the logical subject databases, which will be the foundation for subsequent project work.

Data Administrators generally use data models to communicate their data knowledge. They tend to focus on the conceptual and logical data models and, in data dictionary and CASE tool environments, are effective managers for data objects. In some organizations, they may also be responsible for the physical data models, especially if the Database Administration team uses database-specific tools independent of the organization's CASE tools for database definition.

Process Administration

A limited number of organizations are implementing Process Administration teams to complement their Data Administration function. While Data Administrators focus on the conceptual and logical data models, Process Administrators focus on the conceptual and logical process models. Often linkage objects, such as dataflow diagrams, are the responsibility of Process Administration.

As with Data Administration, the organization has several paths it can take for implementing Process Administration. In one scenario, Process Administration may actually be the applications development resources. They may work on developing the process side of projects, working with the Data Administrators who focus on the data side. Alternatively, Process Administration can be seen as more of a control function, coordinating the use of process objects across projects. In organizations where formal business analysis projects drive actual applications development projects, the Process Administration team may be responsible for the development of the process-oriented portions of the business model.

CASE Tool Support

As organizations begin the implementation of a CASE environment, a group is often established to assist in the implementation across all application development teams. This group typically provides tool assistance and support on a daily basis for the teams. In addition, the group functions as a research and development team, evaluating new CASE tools, features, and technologies.

MODEL MANAGEMENT IMPLEMENTATION ALTERNATIVES

Outlined below are several possible approaches to implementation of a Model Management function in a firm. Each approach has its own set of benefits and drawbacks that may make it appropriate or inappropriate to a firm's environment. The roles of the groups performing the Model Management function differ in each implementation. These alternatives should be evaluated based on the current organizational structure, the goals of the organization, and the desired model management strategy.

Data Administration and Process Administration

For firms with established Data Administration and Process Administration functions, a logical approach to Model Management may be to make the function the joint responsibility of the two groups. The Data Administration team would continue to focus on management of the data objects, while the Process Administration could focus on the process objects. Each team would be responsible for managing their own distinct objects, but would be using a single storage location.

However, by focusing only on pure data or process, the linkages between data and process remain unmanaged. For example, if an Entity Life Cycle Matrix is developed to identify how processes will read and update data, which group will have responsibility for ensuring the integrity of the read and update accesses? If an entity is changed, which group will ensure that all appropriate accesses by processes are appropriately updated? One alternative is to assign this responsibility to Process Administration, since it could be seen as processing logic. However, Data Administration may argue that this was a data change and should therefore be managed by the data team. Clearly defined responsibilities for the use of data in processes must be identified for this approach to be successful.

Data Administration as Model Management

In firms where Process Administration has not yet been established but Data Administration is in place, the Data Administration group will probably be seen as the logical repository administrators. As mentioned earlier, they already have a foundation in many of the skills required for Model Management. However, careful attention must be paid to the current role of Data Administration and how it can effectively expand to include management of all repository objects.

Expansion of the data focus to include complete management of all objects is likely unrealistic. Most Data Administrators have either never been exposed to process objects or have worked very hard to retrain their minds to think with a data, rather than a process, orientation. To effectively manage all process and data objects, they must be retrained to understand the intricacies of process modeling as they understand data modeling. Through this broadening of their scope, the Data Administration group may lose some of their valuable ability to focus on pure data independent of its use. For firms striving to achieve flexible, integrated data design, this refocus may be harmful.

Data Administration with Information Systems Support

One option is to assign responsibility for the integrity of process-related objects to the Information Systems development groups. Data Administration can focus on the management and integrity of data objects and could assist the development groups in the management of their objects. The development groups would work with Data Administration to determine the appropriate level of enterprise-wide encyclopedias. The groups themselves would then be responsible for ensuring integrity of nondata information stored in the repository. As with the Process Administration/Data Administration approach, this option requires the careful identification of responsibility for objects.

Model Management with Separate Data Administration

For firms with an existing Data Administration function, an alternative approach is the establishment of a separate Model Management function. This group would focus on the planning and implementation of the repository for all objects. On a daily basis, the group would ensure the integrity of nondata-oriented objects, while Data Administration would ensure integrity for data objects. Once again, clear definition of data- and nondata-oriented objects would be required to make this implementation effective.

This alternative has several benefits. First, the Data Administration group can maintain its data perspective. This can prove vital to the firm striving toward integrated databases. Second, as Model Management rather than Process Administration, the group is in a position to manage process-oriented objects as well as the linkage between process and data objects. This approach helps achieve a better enterprise-wide perspective for Model Management. This approach allows firms the reusability benefits of both data and process objects while facilitating a strong data management function.

However, the additional workforce requirements of this approach may make its cost prohibitive for many organizations. In some respects there are two functions with some redundancy of skills. If Data Administration plays an active role in the management of data objects in the repository, they are in fact performing many of the same activities as Model Management but are focusing on a different set of objects. Model Management must have some involvement in the change of data objects, since it must validate the appropriate changes to linkages between data and process objects.

An option is to assign Data Administration the role of a data analyst and data designer, but not a manager of the actual objects stored in the repository. This is similar to the concept of the Information Systems developer who is responsible for objects during their development in a project, but is no longer responsible after the completion of a project. In environments where the Data Administration group has not been involved in a traditional data dictionary implementation, it may be feasible to separate the group from repository maintenance. Yet many Data Administration groups may be threatened by what they may perceive as a decrease in power.

Model Management Only

For firms that have not yet established a Data or Process Administration function, a possible implementation may be the establishment of a single Model Management function without a Data Administration function. While this approach will not have the overlapping responsibilities and duplicate skill problems of the other approaches, it will likely not provide the firm with a strong integrated data direction. A major function of Data Administration is to develop and implement a stable, flexible data strategy for the firm that is usable by all systems development. A group focused on Model Management as a whole will likely not emphasize the detailed planning and analysis of data. However, for a firm that accepts or requires project-specific data but would like the flexibility of reusable repository objects, this approach may be optimal.

CASE Tools Support as Model Management

If the establishment of a Model Management group is not feasible and Data and Process Administration have not been established or cannot assume the additional responsibilities of Model

Management, the CASE tool support team may be assigned Model Management responsibility. This group has a distinct advantage in the area of Model Management since they are intimately involved with the specific CASE tools in use at the organization and how they are actually being utilized by the Information Systems teams. Therefore, they understand the essentials of modeling that are required to build the information model for the organization.

Members of the CASE support team are generally closely involved with the projects that are using the tools to develop models. This places this team in the ideal environment to monitor model development throughout the project. From the project team's perspective, the CASE tool support group acts as the single source of project support. Often project team members do not understand the difference between a model management problem and a CASE tool problem.

However, the individuals who are involved in CASE tool support functions tend to be research and development oriented. Model management is at times a tedious function. Often the individuals become frustrated when trying to develop and enforce detailed standards and procedures. They also may lack the business knowledge that is required to understand how models should relate to one another from a nontechnical perspective.

The best results in this scenario may be obtained by selecting one or two individuals within the support group who have the necessary temperament and knowledge of the business to be effective model managers. Allowing these individuals to specialize in Model Management activities may provide better Model Management than expecting the entire support group to perform both support and Model Management functions.

DEVELOPING THE MODEL MANAGEMENT IMPLEMENTATION PLAN

Just as each organization will have its own unique Model Management strategy, it will also have a unique Model Management implementation plan. The critical component of this plan is development of a Model Management team, either by creating a new group or expanding the responsibility of one or more existing teams. The following questions are designed to assist the organization in analyzing its current environment and selecting the most appropriate implementation approach.

Are funds available for a dedicated Model Management staff?

The ideal situation is to create a Model Management staff which is responsible for all Model Management activities at the corporate and project levels. However, most organizations prefer to spend their funds on "productive" resources that actually develop programs; few will have the luxury of a dedicated staff. This means that the goals of Model Management may have to be reduced to be consistent with the available staff size, or alternative organizational locations for Model Management functions need to be identified.

Can the current applications development teams expand their roles to include Model Management without increasing their staff size?

If a complete Model Management staff is not feasible, applications development teams can assume many of the project Model Management functions. Yet these additional responsibilities may overload an already overworked development team. A careful evaluation of the activities currently being performed is required before assigning new tasks to the group.

Although CASE and structured techniques should decrease the total development and maintenance effort over time, experience at most firms has proven that initial projects using CASE tools take at least as long as projects developed using more traditional techniques due to the learning curve involved. Even when teams become proficient and experience the improvement in development time and quality promised by CASE, the tendency is to have them complete more projects instead of spending time effectively managing existing models.

If the applications development teams do have the time to assume the additional responsibility, it is best first to train a team member to be a project model manager. If project models are well developed and conform to a set of standards, it will be easier to combine them at a later date. This assumes that little model reuse and integration will be required.

As teams become proficient in project-level Model Management, some degree of corporate Model Management can be introduced. However, as long as individual application teams remain as model managers, true corporate-wide Model Management is not feasible since there is no one available to consider cross-project issues. However, application-level and perhaps business area-level models could be effectively managed by the applications team.

Is there a Data Administration group?

While the Data Administration group may not be in a position to assume responsibility for all model maintenance, they are likely already performing project and corporate data model maintenance. This reduces the total amount of Model Management effort to be supported. However, it is important to note that Data Administration groups handle only one third of the total Model Management problem. Process and linkage objects still must be effectively controlled.

As mentioned earlier, Data Administration could potentially assume all Model Management responsibility or work in conjunction with applications teams to manage the process and linkage objects. However, organizations electing one of these approaches risk losing some of the benefits of a strong, process-independent, data support team.

Is there a CASE implementation group?

The CASE implementation team has experience in the objects supported by the various CASE tools in use. They can be instrumental in identifying the organization's information model and implementing it into the CASE implementation strategy. However, this group's focus in most organizations is the rapid rollout of advanced tools and techniques. The activities of Model Management are oriented more toward daily control and may not appeal to the research and development mode of many implementation teams. The organization should review the functions of Model Management to identify which, if any, can be effectively performed by the existing individuals in the CASE team. An expansion of the team to include a new individual specifically chosen as model manager may be a compromise.

Is there a Process Administration group?

A Process Administration group, especially in combination with a Data Administration group, can provide the majority of the skills needed for Model Management. This type of group normally focuses on the process and most linkage objects and can therefore provide an effective complement to the Data Administration management of data models. The critical factor in achieving successful Model Management with both Data and Process Administration in place is to clearly identify responsibility for objects and linkages and to define points of coordination.

RECOMMENDED STEPS IN IMPLEMENTING MODEL MANAGEMENT

Step 1: Begin Managing Project Models

Initially, the organization should select an individual to serve as the model manager for one project. This may be someone specifically designated as the corporate model manager or may be a project team member. A member of the Data Administration, Process Administration, or CASE Tool Support group could also be selected if the organization is considering implementing Model Management as a function of one or a combination of these areas.

The goal in this initial project should be to gain an understanding of Model Management concepts. A project information model should be developed and refined as the project team gains an understanding of the models they are developing and how they are actually being used. Some basic standards, such as naming conventions, should be introduced on an experimental basis. Even if these do not develop into the corporate standards, it will be easier to change project models to conform to these standards at a later time if there is some consistency within the models. A basic activity model is also helpful and should be expanded throughout the project as the project model manager learns more about the specific tasks involved.

Once one project has been completed using the Model Management scenario, project team members and management should review the Model Management process for the project. Recommendations on standards, procedures, and Model Management support should be addressed. The results should be used to drive Model Management for several more projects. Each project should include Model Management reviews throughout the project and after implementation.

Model maintenance is a critical issue for model managers. To provide insight into this process, each of the completed project models should be maintained by the project teams. The same individual or a different one may serve as the model manager for maintenance activities. It is important that the project information and activity models be updated throughout this maintenance process since the final corporate Model Management approach must effectively address both development and maintenance.

Teams should be encouraged to use models as review and training documents. This will help identify the types of models that will need to be readily available to the business and Information Systems groups under a variety of scenarios. It may also highlight the need to expand certain types of models and reevaluate the need for other models.

Step 2: Focus on One Set of Objects at the Corporate Level

Before a large number of models are developed by independent teams, the organization needs to begin to control models in a centralized location. To facilitate this higher level of control, the organization should practice on a small subset of the models. This subset could be a group of related objects, such as all logical data objects, or could be a set of project models, such as all projects that support a specific business area. The initial subset should be as small as possible, but must cross at least two project models.

At this point, the organization needs to select an individual to serve as the corporate model manager. Based on the issues raised in this chapter and the experiences gained at the project level, the organization should be able to select the organizational location or locations of the Model Management function and identify the correct individual for the job. During this experimental phase, one individual should be sufficient, but a backup person who is involved in the research would be beneficial.

In merging project models into a corporate model, the model manager will gain experience in the CASE tool, how it handles merging, any cross-tool issues, and reconciling model differences. Although not all problem areas can be identified, it will provide the model manager with an understanding of the major issues and how to handle them. Management can gain critical insights into the amount of time that will be required for corporate-level Model Management.

Once the initial subset has been combined, the model manager either may elect to perform more research by continuing to combine models or may evaluate the levels of corporate repositories that are appropriate to the organization. More experimentation into merging the organization's models may be required before a recommendation on repository levels can be reached. However, significant problems in combining simple models may cause the model manager to recommend limited corporate-wide repositories at this time.

Initial corporate Model Management standards and procedures can now be developed. These may affect the standards and procedures for ongoing project models and thus should be carefully implemented. It may be wise to have these standards apply only to new projects. Model managers then have the option of converting existing project models to the new standards after completion.

Step 3: Gradually Expand the Focus to Include All Project Models at the Appropriate Corporate Level

With a first cut at the repository levels, standards, and procedures, the model manager is ready to begin corporate-wide Model Management. If many models have already been developed, it will take a while for all models to be combined to the appropriate level.

This merging should be done gradually, each time encompassing more project models or more types of objects across all projects.

Once a set of models is available at the appropriate corporate level, the Model Management group can begin to experiment with support for model reuse across projects. Up to this point, reuse has likely been limited to a specific project since project teams did not know what models were available to them. The first experiment in coordinating model use across projects should be limited to a model that can be easily verified to be correct—for example, physical data models that can always be compared to or generated from the production file layouts. This should be a model that will be updated by both project teams so that the sharing of model changes can be tested.

Once a system of model change management has been established, the Model Management team is ready to begin full Model Management. The standards and procedures should be expanded to include reuse issues. At this point, the Model Management team has probably been expanded to support all Model Management activities, and the team members are actively involved in supporting project teams and model inquiries on a daily basis.

Glossary of Model Management Terms

Activity Model   A model that diagrams the activities performed by model management and how those activities manage specific repository objects.

Analysis Phase   The phase in the systems development life cycle when the requirements of the business are analyzed and major components of a system are identified from a business perspective.

Application   A grouping of programs and supporting data structures.

Attribute   A detailed piece of information that describes an entity. Examples are Customer Name and Product Identifier.

Business Area   A way of grouping business functions based on organizational structure.

CASE   Computer Aided Systems Engineering or Computer Aided Software Engineering. The process of analyzing the business and building supporting systems through the use of structured techniques, including modeling.

CASE Tool   A tool that supports CASE activities.

Conceptual Model   A high-level model that illustrates information, processes, or their interaction.

Construction Phase   The phase in the systems development life cycle when the actual programs are coded and tested and the physical database is built and populated. Also includes implementation activities.

Corporate Model   A model that applies across the organization. Many include many project models.

Dataflow   The flow of information between a data store or external agent and a process. Represented in a dataflow diagram.

Data Model   A model that diagrams information used by the business. May be specific to an information system.

Data Store   A group of stored information that is either sent to or received from a process. Represented in a dataflow diagram.

Design Phase   The phase in the systems development life cycle when the details of an information system are defined. Major activities include screen and report design and specification development.

Entity   A group of information that represents a person, place, object, or concept of interest to the business. Examples are Customer, Warehouse, Product, Forecast.

Entity Life Cycle Matrix   A cross reference between entities and processes that describes how each process accesses the entity.

Entity Relationship   The key-based relationship between two entities. Represents business rules. Examples are A Customer has many Orders, A Price is for one and only one Product.

External Agent   An object, organizational group or system that is outside the boundary of the system or business area but that receives information from or sends information to the business or system. Represented in a dataflow diagram.

Information Model   A model that diagrams the objects stored in the repository, their relationships to each other, and the detailed information tracked about them.

Linkage Model   A model that diagrams how information is used by specific processes. May be specific to an information system.

Logical Model A model of information used by the business, processes performed by the business or a system, or the interaction between data and processes. This model includes more detail than the conceptual model but does not include the technical perspective of the physical model.

Lower CASE A tool that supports the design and construction activities of the project life cycle.

Matrix A cross reference between two types of objects. Usually applies to a cross reference between a data object and a process object.

Model A representation of information, business processes, system processes, or their interaction. May be graphical or textual.

Model Management The process of coordinating the use and maintenance of models across multiple users, including project teams and individuals within the business.

Object A component of a model. An object is stored in a repository.

Physical Model A model that diagrams a physical database, program or module, screen or report. Includes technical considerations.

Planning Phase The phase in the systems development life cycle when the needs of the business are determined and an information system or set of systems are identified to meet the needs.

Process A function or activity performed by the business or by an information system. Represented in a process model.

Process Model A model that diagrams the functions or activities performed by the business or by an information system.

Project Model A model that is developed by, and/or used by, a specific project. A project may be a business analysis, planning, systems development, or maintenance project.

Report Layout A representation of a report and its components.

Repository   A centralized storage location for models.

Screen Layout   A representation of a screen and its components.

Specification   A set of processing logic. It may refer to a program, a module, or a process.

Subject Area   A way of grouping sets of data based on business definitions.

Upper CASE   A tool that supports the earlier phases of the project life cycle, including planning, analysis, and early design.

Index